FEAR
LEARNING TO COPE

LEARNING TO COPE

By
Albert G. Forgione, Ph.D.
Richard S. Surwit, Ph.D.

with
Daniel G. Page

VNR VAN NOSTRAND REINHOLD COMPANY
NEW YORK   CINCINNATI   ATLANTA   DALLAS   SAN FRANCISCO
LONDON   TORONTO   MELBOURNE

Allen County Public Library
Ft. Wayne, Indiana

Van Nostrand Reinhold Company Regional Offices:
New York   Cincinnati   Atlanta   Dallas   San Francisco

Van Nostrand Reinhold Company International Offices:
London   Toronto   Melbourne

Copyright © 1978 by Litton Educational Publishing, Inc.

Library of Congress Catalog Card Number: 77-17029
ISBN: 0-442-26388-0

Manufactured in the United States of America

Published by Van Nostrand Reinhold Company
450 West 33rd Street, New York. N.Y. 10001

Published simultaneously in Canada by Van Nostrand Reinhold Ltd.

15 14 13 12 11 10 9 8 7 6 5 4 3 2 1

Library of Congress Cataloging in Publication Data
Forgione, Albert G
    Fear.

    1. Fear. 2. Peace of mind. I. Surwit, Richard S.,
joint author. II. Page, Daniel G., joint author.
III. Title.
BF575.F2F67   158'.1   77-17029
ISBN 0-442-26388-0

Preface

Fear: Learning to Cope is a layman's guide to the understanding and treatment of fear. Its emphasis is strongly on self-help. Unlike many popular psychology books, the ideas dealt with in this book are not the personal speculations of the authors. Rather, the theory and methods that we have outlined owe their conception to some fifty years of research on the nature and treatment of common behavioral problems.

We have not written an academic book, and so in places we have taken the liberty of simplifying some of the complexities of psychological theory for the sake of clarity. Because each chapter draws upon information presented in previous chapters, we urge you to read the book in its entirety before attempting to apply any of the techniques to a specific, personal fear problem. Reading individual chapters out of context will only be confusing, and trying to use isolated bits and pieces of the techniques proposed here will almost certainly prove futile. The book presents a unified set of concepts that must be applied systematically and in concert to be effective.

Early chapters discuss what fear is, how it works against us, and how it affects our lives. The behavioral approach is defined and briefly compared with earlier psychoanalytic theories. We introduce the basic philosophy of our approach and, in later chapters, present easy-to-follow, step-by-step instructions on how to tackle personal fear-related problems. The reader is taught how to relax and how to use relaxation to combat fear. Further chapters then enlarge upon specific techniques for controlling obsessive thoughts, for developing more assertive social behaviors, and for dealing with compulsive problems. The closing chapters focus on some of the most common types of fear. Throughout, we have used case histories to illustrate how the techniques presented can be applied to overcome fear.

Just as *Fear: Learning to Cope* is not intended as a textbook, it should also not be considered as a substitute for professional assistance when such assistance is required. We have taken special care to point out along the way when the reader should consider obtaining professional help. For many fears, the reader will find that the knowledge provided by this book will be sufficient to allow an effective self-help approach. For more severe fears and phobias, self-help will need to be augmented by a structured, intensive program under professional guidance. If you have a fear problem, you may well find that by gaining a better understanding of the nature of fear and the techniques available for dealing with it, you will be in a better position to benefit from professional assistance, should it be required, in the process of learning to cope.

ALBERT G. FORGIONE
RICHARD S. SURWIT

Contents

LEARNING TO COPE

1.
WE ALL HAVE FEARS

If you met Ted R., you would probably like him. Most people do. He has a warm, outgoing manner and a good sense of humor. A successful salesman in his mid-thirties, Ted is a good husband and father. He is an outdoors enthusiast and especially enjoys skiing, mountain climbing, and white-water canoeing.

You would never think of Ted as neurotic or overly fearful. Yet, like the rest of us, Ted has fears. He is particularly afraid of flying. When his business requires him to travel away from his suburban home outside Boston, he drives. At vacation time, his family always goes to places that can be easily reached by car.

Ted does not say that he is afraid to fly. He simply says that he "doesn't like to fly." In that way, he avoids being kidded or ridiculed. Ted can give any number of good reasons for his aversion to flying: he doesn't want to get into the rat race of a heavy travel schedule; driving is more economical; he doesn't have to waste time waiting around airports; and he never has to wonder where his luggage is. He has recited these reasons so often that he almost believes them. While these reasons reflect certain attitudes that Ted holds, they have nothing whatsoever to do with his refusal to fly.

When Ted's company had a chance to make a large sale in the Midwest, Ted was selected to close the deal. It was an opportunity that offered him recognition and prestige within the company, along with a sizable commission. Ted was naturally flattered at

1

being chosen. But he began to suggest reasons why someone else might be a better choice. Perhaps it would be more impressive to have one of the vice presidents make the call. Perhaps one of the sales engineers would have a better technical understanding of the customer's needs. The objections were ignored and simply regarded as modesty on Ted's part.

On the day before he was to fly to Cleveland, Ted called his boss. He had come down with the flu. The company would have to send someone in his place. His boss called back half an hour later with some good news. He had called the prospective customer in Cleveland, and the customer was perfectly agreeable to postponing the visit for a week—plenty of time for Ted to recover.

When the day came for Ted to leave, his boss drove him to the airport, even though Ted insisted that it was not necessary. At the airport, as soon as Ted's boss had departed, Ted hailed a cab, rushed home to pick up his car, and, in a grueling twenty-four-hour marathon, drove straight through to Cleveland. He was only forty-five minutes late for his appointment the next day.

Ted's decision to drive to Cleveland was not based on any of his good reasons for not liking to fly. He knew that no imaginable inconvenience of air travel could match the physical and mental strain of a nonstop, round-the-clock drive. Since Ted's company was paying for the trip, the higher cost of flying was not a factor in his decision. As for safety, Ted was well aware that driving in a badly fatigued condition was much more dangerous than flying. Even the most avid nonfliers are usually aware that serious or fatal accidents are far more likely to occur in an automobile than an airplane.

The simple truth for Ted, and for hundreds of thousands like him, is that fear alone kept him from flying. Given a choice between being placed in a fear-provoking situation or enduring the strain, discomfort, and hardship of a nonfearful alternative, he chose to avoid the fear. And rather than risk looking foolish for being afraid, he chose to conceal his fear. Such is the overwhelming and irrational power that fear can hold over our lives.

Fortunately for Ted R. and all those like him, the story does not end here. We will meet Ted again in Chapter 12.

Elaine M. is afraid to leave her house. She is an attractive woman of energy, talent, and intelligence. Not long ago, she was very active as a spokeswoman for women's groups and local civic organizations. When Elaine first began to cut back on her busy schedule, she explained that she felt the need to be a better mother to her ten-year-old daughter and eight-year-old son. She dropped the activities that took her farthest from home, but for a while remained active in the local PTA and the League of Women Voters. Later she dropped even those activities.

Elaine is a loving mother who indeed values the time she spends with her children. But with both children in school for much of the day, she need not have stopped the outside activities that she found so rewarding and fulfilling. The real reason she has dropped out is *fear*. She misses her outside activities desperately and fully recognizes the irrationality of giving them up. But this mysterious and unaccountable fear so dominates her that she believes she has no choice but to avoid it in the only way she knows—by not setting foot outside her house.

Ted and Elaine are not unusual. In fact, they are pretty average in many respects. Although fear makes them behave in ways that are inappropriate, their strategies for coping with fear are fairly typical. Probably each of us at some time has experienced, in varying degrees, fear similar to that which beset Ted and Elaine. Fear is a universal human experience. Equally common is irrational and ineffective human behavior for coping with fear.

Psychology textbooks list more than 180 different kinds of fear. In addition to fear of flying in airplanes and going away from home, other common fears include fear of being in cramped spaces or high places, receiving medical treatment, going to the dentist, having sex, and many more—all complete with mysterious Latin names. Often, fears are related to very specific situations, such as riding in elevators, going through tunnels, having teeth drilled, or speaking in front of a group. People will often fear something in one particular situation only: for instance, a person who is afraid of heights in an office building may have no similar fear when standing atop a mountain. Some airline pilots have been known to have a fear of heights—except while they were flying. The types of fears that exist and the situations that people are afraid of are as numerous as the individuals who suffer from such fears.

HIDING OUR FEARS

If fear is as common as we suggest, why don't we see everyone running around in a state of continual panic? One reason is that people quickly learn to manage their lives in such a way that they avoid the situations they fear. Avoidance can sometimes be maintained without sacrificing other aspects of our lives that are important to us. More often, however, avoidance behavior interferes with doing things that are valued (Elaine's outside activities), or else it forces us into situations that have more real danger (Ted's driving in a state of exhaustion) than the one that is feared.

Most of us become masters of speaking and thinking in ways that hide our fears from others and from ourselves. Recall that Ted says he does not like to fly. With this single handy phrase he can bypass the entire issue without having to confront the simple truth that he is afraid to fly. Negative attitudes may often be the only visible sign of a hidden fear.

Recall also that Ted can give a number of "rational explanations" for not liking to fly. Elaine is also adept at rationalizing, saying that she stays at home because she wants to be a better mother. From early childhood on, we learn to build walls of reason that keep our fears private and out of sight from all but the most determined observers.

In our everyday speech, we use expressions that make fear seem to be a loud, violent, and highly visible phenomenon. People *scream* in terror, are *sick* with fear, and *petrified* with fright. True, these outward signs may accompany our experience of fear. But just as there are all different kinds of fears, so are there all degrees of fear. For the most part, fears exact their toll of human suffering in tension-filled silence.

The executive who spends twelve hours a day at the office and then brings work home at night may behave that way in order to ward off a strong fear of failure. The timid child who won't speak in front of adults or the blushing adolescent who cannot summon the courage to ask for a date is perhaps showing fear of rejection. These "quiet fears" act on us in insidious ways. Even though they can be as devastating as their more visible counterparts, society's reaction to these fears is very different. We chide the shy child. We say the adolescent will grow out of it. We even praise the fear-driven workaholic for having ambition.

There is a final reason why fear may not be more obvious. We may be looking for the wrong things. Unlike measles with its telltale red spots, fear is not a sickness and has no unique identifying symptoms. People with fears are not mentally deranged, and they usually do not act in ways that set them apart. As the stories of Ted and Elaine illustrate, people with fears are, for the most part, involved with things other than their fears—jobs, outside activities, and other people. They are no different from people that you know—friends, family, perhaps you yourself.

AVOIDING FEARS, CREATING PROBLEMS

Some fears are useful. They have survival value. They help us to adapt our behavior in situations where real danger is present. Adaptive fears keep us out of harm's way by instilling in us a tendency to avoid situations that truly threaten our lives, our health, or our happiness.

Adaptive fears do not create problems for us. But if we are afraid when there is no real danger, our fear is misplaced. Such misplaced fears keep us from achieving our full potential. They get in the way of our enjoyment of life, make us uncomfortable, interfere with our jobs, strain our relations with other people, and cause us to feel inadequate. Misplaced fears stunt our lives, sometimes overwhelming us so that they become the focal point of our lives. They become crippling. When we try to control our misplaced fears by avoiding them, we are often forced to adopt patterns of behavior that are unproductive, joyless, even dangerous.

Attempts to control misplaced fears by avoiding them is a little bit like a silly vaudeville routine in which the patient tells the doctor, "It hurts to raise my hand over my head." The doctor replies, "So don't raise your hand over your head." Such advice is plainly absurd, but it leads to an interesting question. What is wrong with avoidance behavior if it holds our fear in check? For some fears, the answer is obvious. If being afraid of the dentist keeps you from taking care of an abscessed tooth, you risk serious consequences for your health. If sexual fears lead to frustration and loss of self-esteem, the penalty may be the destruction of a potentially happy sex life.

For other fears, the problems of avoidance behavior are less obvious, although no less acute in terms of human suffering. Being afraid to fly may not sound especially serious. It seems relatively easy to choose not to fly—unless your livelihood depends on long-distance traveling. Fear of flying is no trivial matter if it means not seeing loved ones who live far away, or having to give up vacations to places you long to visit. Fear is a problem if the enjoyment of watching a movie turns to panic at the sight of an airplane taking off.

And flying is not an isolated example. If you are afraid of elevators, it might seem simple enough to avoid them— unless you have a heart condition, or work on the forty-eighth floor of the World Trade Center, or earn your living as an elevator operator. If you are afraid of flying insects, you can put screens on your windows. But forget about picnics. And avoid taking walks in the spring and summer. Our lives simply cannot be rich and full if they are spent avoiding misplaced fears of dogs, highways, the dark—and the list goes on, endlessly.

Fear makes us trade down in our scale of values. To avoid fear, we give up aspects of our lives that we truly value and enjoy—and we get only diminished self-esteem in return. If we could secure some measure of happiness, security, or peace of mind by avoiding fear, the trade might almost seem fair. What we get from avoidance, however, is more fear—fear of showing our fear, fear that the walls we have built around our fear are not high enough or strong enough to keep it under control and out of sight.

Avoidance behavior, in effect, feeds the fear. By failing to confront the fear, we fail to learn how to master it, and we create a climate in which other fears may grow and multiply.

LEARNING TO CONTROL FEARS

Three themes are interwoven throughout this book. The first is that we all have misplaced fears. Regardless of how original or unique we think our specific fears are, we are certain to discover that we are actually part of a community of fellow phobics. Misplaced fear makes us feel cut off from the rest of the world, but it is in fact one of the most widely shared of all human experiences.

Our second theme is that fear is not a cause for shame or embarrassment. There is no need to keep our fears hidden from ourselves or from others. A basic rule of psychology is that we cannot control anything unless we are consciously aware of it. We need to bring our fears into the open as an important first step in learning to cope effectively with them—which brings us to our third theme: you can learn to control your fear. Controlling fear is not the same as hiding it. A person who endures fear in stoic, tight-lipped silence is not controlling fear, but is being controlled by it. Control means far more than not screaming, crying, running away, vomiting, or inadvertently urinating.

You are in control when you yourself take command of the situation. You exercise power over the thoughts and images in your mind and diminish the emotion of fear. You command your muscles when to tense and when to relax. When *you* decide whether to meet a fearful situation either by fighting, running, or sitting back and relaxing, then *you* are in control of your fear.

This book is organized along lines that we believe are most useful in helping people learn to control their fears. We start by developing a better understanding of the nature of fears and the ways they affect our thoughts, our bodies, and our lives. We seek to dispel some of the mystery that surrounds both fear and its treatment.

In a simple, step-by-step approach, we present specific techniques that you can use to deal with fear. These techniques are based on modern behavioral research and clinical practice. The techniques work, and, with some practice, you can learn to use them.

Just why some of these techniques work is not always understood in the strictest scientific sense, and we do not try to unravel any academic tangles in this book. We present some theory where it seems to be plausible and fairly well accepted. But theoretical considerations are treated primarily as background against which to view techniques for learning to control fears.

We include some information on how fears arise, not because we feel that knowing the cause of fear is particularly useful in coping with it, but rather because some knowledge in this area can help us avoid creating or intensifying fears in others.

Finally, we close with several chapters that illustrate how the coping techniques can be applied to specific fears. These chapters also explain some of the methods that psychologists use in behavior therapy. If the self-treatment that we present does not work for you, these other avenues of help are available.

We believe that this volume can help people with mild and moderate fear problems to learn to become better self-managers. These are the people who for one reason or another would probably not seek professional help. For people with more intense fear problems, this book introduces them to some of the types of help available and some of the techniques that professional therapists use. We hope that this will encourage people who feel the need for professional help to seek it.

This is not intended to be an academic textbook about fear. Our efforts are aimed at reaching people and helping them to free their lives from the unpleasant consequences of misplaced fears.

2.
THE NATURE OF FEAR

What we believe is usually an outgrowth of what we have been taught, what we have learned, and our knowledge in general. By changing the state of our knowledge, we can also change the state of our beliefs. The purpose of this chapter and the next one is to begin the process of changing your beliefs about fear. We will do this by setting into motion a number of learning processes that will provide you with new knowledge about the nature of fear, about the way people react to fears, and about ways of coping with fears.

A large part of the learning process will involve learning and practicing new forms of behavior. You will start by learning to behave calmly in nonstressful situations. Then, by very gradually increasing the stress under which you practice calm behavior, you will gradually change your beliefs—because you will find out that you can be relaxed in situations that were once stressful for you. When the learning process is complete, you will have new knowledge about how to cope with fears. You will have new expectations about how you will react to fear-provoking situations. Most importantly, you will have new forms of behavior that let you remain calm, relaxed, and totally in control of situations that formerly produced fear and panic.

We begin this new learning process by tracing several common threads that run through the wide varieties of fear. As we begin to weave these threads into a more unified concept, we expect to accomplish three things.

First, we will make fear less of an unknown quantity. Since the unknown is itself a source of fear, we can make some immediate progress just by getting rid of some of the mystery and misinformation that surround fear and by replacing them with facts.

Second, we will acquaint you with ways in which people learn to be afraid. We will show how you can turn these same learning mechanisms to your advantage in the learning of nonfearful behavior.

Third, understanding the general nature of fear will help you to understand why the specific techniques presented in later chapters are effective. Without this basic understanding, the methods that we propose may sound like a sorcerer's incantations. We want you to understand that the techniques are directly and scientifically related to your ability to cope with fear. If you know *what the techniques are and why they work,* you will be more inclined to make the effort to learn and practice new behaviors for dealing with fear.

SEEDS OF FEAR

If you drop a young animal, it will immediately spread out its body so that its weight is as widely distributed as possible when it lands. This reflexive response protects the animal by giving it a better chance to survive a fall. Many such reflexes are innate. Humans are born with them, and they have survival value.

Certain of our fears appear to be directly related to inborn reflexes. Sudden changes, loud noises, and high places all evoke fearful responses in newborn children. Some higher mammals exhibit an innate fear of deformed faces or dismembered bodies.

In addition to innate fears, most young children show varying degrees of fear to furry animals (e.g., dogs, cats, mice), snakes, darkness, being closed in, and being left alone. These fears do not appear to be inborn. Rather, we learn them. And, judging by the large number of people who have such fears, they must be very easily learned. By contrast, people are almost never afraid of rocks or trees or tables.

It is easy to see why some things are more easily feared than others. In our normal experience we simply don't usually encounter chairs that shock us, rocks that jump up at us, or trees that make loud, sudden noises. We frequently encounter dogs that make sudden lunges, spaces in which we are uncomfortably crowded, and dark rooms where we can't see what's going on. In other words, easily learned fears occur in situations where there is likely to be high arousal.

Innate fears and easily learned fears are the seeds from which phobias grow. This fact partially accounts for the difficulty of overcoming phobias. There is nearly always a rational basis for the phobia because it can be related to survival *(If I fall from a high place I'll be killed)* or to avoiding common dangers *(Some dogs bite)*. A problem of course occurs when these seeds are allowed to grow out of control and to thus assume a role in our lives that is disproportionate to any threat that actually exists. The seeds of fear serve us well as reminders to be on our guard in certain situations. Allowed to grow and multiply unchecked, however, they can permeate and stifle our entire life.

Let us now turn our attention to the ways in which we cultivate these seeds of fear through learning processes.

LEARNING BY ASSOCIATION

Mark, a nineteen-year-old college student, stayed up most of the night, cramming for a biology exam. The next day, Mark was tired and anxious to do well. As he was on his way to take the test, the science-building elevator in which Mark was riding became stuck between floors. He immediately became concerned that he would miss the class. The elevator was crowded with students, some of whom began to shout and to bang on the door to attract attention. As the din around him increased, Mark suddenly began to feel uncomfortably warm. He was so hot that he feared the building might be on fire. His hands began to tremble, he could hardly breathe, and his heart was pounding furiously. His palms were sweating so profusely that his notebook almost slipped out of his grasp. Within minutes, the minor electrical fault that had caused the delay was repaired and the elevator resumed operation. But the incident had left a deep impression on Mark.

For the next two weeks he did not use the elevator but walked up eight flights of stairs instead. Then one morning he was running behind schedule and was tired from having again studied late the night before. When he arrived at the science building, he decided to try the elevator once more. Although the elevator operated normally, each little noise that he heard on the way up sent him into panic. Every time the elevator stopped at a floor, Mark was sure it had become stuck again. He became concerned that his fear was obvious to the others on the elevator, which made matters even worse. Mark was pale and shaken when he stepped out. Thereafter, he always took the stairs in the science building, regardless of how late or tired he was.

Several days later, on a warm spring afternoon, Mark was on his way to an interview for a summer job. The employment office was on the sixteenth floor and since Mark did not want to be perspiring and out of breath when he applied for a job, he took the elevator. It was a cranky old piece of equipment that shuddered and bumped with every stop or start. It was more than Mark could take. He got off at the tenth floor, angry and ashamed at having let the feeling of fear overpower him. The learning process was complete. Mark had developed a full-fledged "elevator fear," and, from then on, he consistently refused to ride in elevators.

Mark had the misfortune of being exposed several times in a relatively brief period to a perfect learning situation for which he was the perfectly prepared pupil. The pattern was roughly the same in each case. When he rode the elevator, something happened to frighten him. The fear that he experienced one time in a single faulty elevator in the science building became a generalized fear of all elevators. Through the process of association, he had come to expect that each time he rode in an elevator something frightening would occur. And he was not disappointed in his expectations.

Mark was exceptionally vulnerable to learning a fear in each of the three situations. He was physically tired, anxious about the test or the interview, and his usual coping defenses were not up to the added strain of any new anxiety. As Figure 2-1 shows, the combined effects of a high level of anxiety and an intense specific arousal pushed Mark above the stress level at which he was normally capable of coping. Had he been less anxious to start with, the initial bad experience could have fallen within his normal range of tolerances and might have produced no more than a passing annoyance.

This type of learning is similar to classical conditioning; the principle involved is one of association. When a particular response typically follows a given stimulus, we

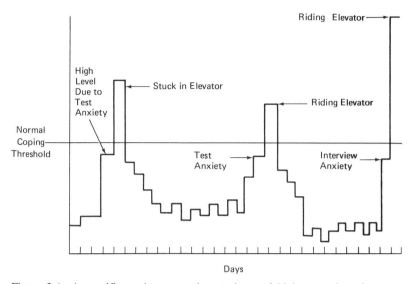

Figure 2-1. A specific anxiety occurring at times of high general **anxiety** can create fears by exceeding the normal level at which a person can cope **with** the situation.

begin to associate the two, even if they have no logical or necessary connection.

The discovery of this type of learning by association was made by a Russian physiologist named Ivan Pavlov. Pavlov was conducting experiments on digestion and salivation in dogs. Tubes inserted in an animal's mouth and stomach extracted digestive fluids as they were secreted. Pavlov became intrigued by a puzzling phenomenon. At first, a dog would salivate only when food was placed in its mouth. After a few trials, the dog would begin to salivate at the sight of a food dish. And before long, the dog would salivate at the sound of the experimenter's approaching footsteps.

Realizing that he had stumbled upon something considerably more important than a simple fact about digestion in dogs, Pavlov undertook a series of experiments in which a bell was sounded, a dog was presented with food, and an experimenter noted when the dog began to salivate. After only a few trials, the dogs learned to associate the bell with the food; they salivated as soon as they heard it. Of particular interest was that, even when Pavlov stopped following the bell with food, the dogs would continue to salivate at the sound of the bell. They had learned a particular behavior in a particular situation, and they continued to use that newly learned behavior even when it was no longer appropriate.

In addition to showing the powerful link that association forges between a stimulus and a response, Pavlov's experiments demonstrated that learning by association affects the autonomic nervous system. By controlling the so-called involuntary functions of the body—such as heart rate, blood pressure, perspiration, respiration, tension in the smooth muscles, and salivation—the autonomic nervous system exerts a tremendous effect on what we actually experience when we are afraid. Thus, Pavlov's discovery that learning can alter the state of these involuntary functions has profound importance for understanding and treating fear problems.

Psychological experiments have shown that classical conditioning, or learning by association, can be used to teach people to be afraid of anything. A simple example of this is hooking up a chair so that it delivers an electric shock whenever a person sits down. Very quickly, the person associates the discomfort of the shock with the chair, and becomes afraid to sit down in it.

While such experiments show that people can learn to fear virtually anything, given the right conditions, they also show that people are inclined to fear some objects more than others. For example, a person with a basic mistrust of small furry animals will learn to fear a cat in fewer trials than it takes for a a person to learn to fear a chair. People who learn to fear chairs in laboratory experiments typically do not generalize the fear to all chairs. They seem to learn very quickly to distinguish chairs in the laboratory that shock them from chairs in the real world that don't. Also, fears of inanimate objects and innately nonfearful situations must be learned under unusual conditions. Once the startling stimuli are stopped and the manufactured learning conditions removed, these artificial fears tend to go away rather quickly and of their own accord.

Learning by association helps to explain why some objects are more easily feared than others. When a cat scratches a man, the man blames the cat. If scratched often enough or severely enough, the man will possibly begin to fear cats. Animals have a capacity for unexpected behavior that can startle or hurt us. Inanimate objects, on the other hand, have no such capacity. Thus, although we recognize that a thrown rock can hurt us, we associate the hurt with the thrower and not the rock.

If simple awareness of the association between stimulus and response were enough to keep us from learning fear, then coping with phobias would be simple indeed. However, awareness is only a first step. Without learning new behaviors to replace fearful responses, the fear will persist. A famous psychological experiment casts an interesting light on the relationship of awareness to the learning of fears.

The experimenter set out to discover if he could deliberately make himself afraid. Each time he encountered a man with bright red hair, he acted afraid—he would simulate startle responses, run away, and seek to avoid coming across red-headed men. Before long, he had so thoroughly assimilated this behavior into his normal patterns of response that he began to spontaneously exhibit actual symptoms of genuine fear. The mechanisms of fear that are somehow built into our unconscious processes appear to be far stronger than the simple awareness of the conscious mind.

Before turning to other forms of learning, we should consider briefly a special case of learning by association—*trauma*. People often believe that fears are the outgrowth of a traumatic childhood experience. Trauma is essentially a case of classical conditioning in which the single coupling of an object (or event) with an accompanying response is so strong that the association is forged on the basis of that single happening. Traumatic experiences are by no means the major cause of phobias. Because we tend to remember vividly a traumatic experience, we may mistakenly regard it as the "cause of a fear," when in fact it is only one of many associative links by which the fear was learned.

LEARNING BY REWARDS

Marian and Mike are an attractive married couple in their early thirties. Mike is a successful public relations executive who spends much of his time organizing and attending parties, fund-raising balls, and conventions for his clients. He likes Marian to go to these functions with him. At first, it all seemed exciting and new. Later on, when the novelty of going to so many big events started to wear off, she wished she could spend more time at home. She tried to convince Mike that she should stay home but he was insistent, so she continued to go in order to please him. One night, at a fund-raising rally for a political candidate, a group of demonstrators forced their way into the hall and began to create a disturbance. Several scuffles broke out in the crowd.

Although Marian was not hurt, she was shoved around a little and was frightened. Mike was completely sympathetic and took her home right away. For the rest of the week, he was unusually attentive to her and did everything he could to comfort her after the unpleasant experience.

The next weekend, Marian reluctantly agreed to attend another function. A couple of times during the evening, when the crowd became unusually noisy, Marian told Mike that it made her nervous. He responded by putting his arm around her and paying special attention to her. A few days later Marian told her husband that she didn't want to go with him to a cocktail party because the crowds were becoming too much for her. He suggested that she stay home and take it easy.

During the next several months, Marian frequently complained that crowds made her feel confined and frightened. The first time it happened, Mike brought her home early. Later, he became irritated and said she was just being silly. She cried and said she didn't want to be afraid, but she was so terrified that she simply couldn't bear to be in large groups of people. Eventually, Mike stopped asking her to go with him. As a result, she was able to avoid contact with crowds much of the time. On those few occasions when she couldn't find a way out, she would try to get as far away from people as possible. She would sit in tight-lipped silence trying to hold back the waves of panic that swept over her.

Marian had learned her lesson too well. She had developed a fearful behavior that rewarded her by allowing her to avoid the constant round of events and by increasing the amount of attention that she received from her husband. Marian learned fear through a principle known as *instrumental conditioning*. Whereas classical conditioning teaches us to associate a particular stimulus with a response, instrumental conditioning teaches us to associate a stimulus with a form of behavior for which we are rewarded. The reward may be external to us (as when Mike showed increased attention to Marian) or it may be internal (as when we do something because it feels good, such as when

Marian stayed away from the parties). The principle of instrumental conditioning is illustrated in Figure 2-2.

As the figure shows, the reward reinforces the response, which leads to further reward, in a closed loop. Numerous experiments have confirmed that any response followed by a favorable outcome increases the frequency of the response.

Applied specifically to the learning of fear, the principle of instrumental conditioning can be illustrated as in Figure 2-3. As the figure shows, the seed of fear must be present to begin with. A form of behavior follows. If the behavior leads to a reward, the behavior is reinforced. In other words, the next time the feared object or situation is encountered, there is a better chance that the behavior that caused the fear to be reduced before will be repeated. In the case of Marian and Mike, Marian's behavior was being rewarded in two ways. Whenever she complained about being afraid in a crowd, Mike was more attentive to her. Unintentionally, he was rewarding her behavior and helping her learn to be afraid. At the same time, her fear of crowds gave her an opportunity to stay away from some of the parties, which she wanted to do anyway. Through this dual reinforcement, a small fear, which began as little more than a minor discomfort, was nurtured into a phobia. In this scenario lie the seeds of a tragedy: as Marian's fears demand more of Mike's attention and make her increasingly

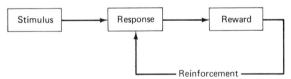

Figure 2-2. Through instrumental conditioning, we associate a particular behavioral response with a reward, which in turn reinforces the response.

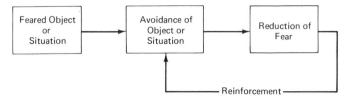

Figure 2-3. Instrumental conditioning applied to the learning of a fear.

unable to live up to his social requirements, he may well reach a point when he will reject her.

We express a fear, and a well-meaning friend reinforces it by telling us of someone else with a similar fear, offering to protect us from the fear, or making us feel important by showering us with attention. Similarly, we find ourselves faced with a disagreeable task, part of which may contain a small element of fear. It might be going to work in a subway, or walking past some rowdy dogs, or having a tooth pulled. We find some handy excuse to avoid doing the task, and are rewarded with a reduction in anxiety. Faced with that same situation the next time, it is easier for us to avoid doing it, because we are starting to learn that we can make ourselves feel better—momentarily at least—by our avoidance.

One of the best and surest ways to keep instrumental conditioning from blowing our fears out of proportion, is to meet these minor fears head-on. People learning to ride horses are often told that if they fall off, they must immediately get back on. Like many bits of folk wisdom, this one is backed by solid psychological principles. Getting back on the horse does not permit avoidance behavior with its attendant reward of fear reduction. In other words, instrumental conditioning is not allowed to take over. The initial discomfort of facing up to minor fears is small indeed in comparison to the far-reaching impact that a phobia can exercise over our lives.

LEARNING BY IMITATION

Seven-year-old Brenda is flying out to California with her mother. Throughout the entire trip, she will hear her mother worry about missing the flight; getting on the wrong plane; not being able to get off the ground with so many people on the plane; not being able to land because of bad weather; lack of fuel; a drunken pilot; not being able to find their way around the airport once they arrive; and not being able to find the plane to come home on. The mother's fear is contagious and will probably plant the seed of fear in Brenda's mind. There is a good chance that when Brenda is old enough to travel on her own, she will adopt the behavior patterns of her mother. She too will be afraid to fly.

All people—and children in particular—learn to do a great many things by watching others and imitating their actions. In fact, imitation may be the most common form of learning. It is common to all higher primates, it is a fast way of learning, and it is quite often adaptive—it has survival value. In some cases, we consciously fix upon an admired individual and model ourselves after him or her. More often, we unconsciously and uncritically adopt certain traits of people with whom we are in frequent contact. In this way, we sometimes imitate fearful behavior. We may simply assume (or unconsciously accept) that since Mr. or Ms. X does something this way, it must be the right way. Having hit upon a way of doing whatever that something is, we don't bother to find out if it's the right way or even the best way.

If we learn fearful behavior from a person whom we

admire, we often learn at the same time how to rationalize this behavior to make it acceptable. If a friend tells us that he is afraid of flying because his uncle was once in a plane crash, we might accept that reason as our own for being afraid to fly.

Even if we don't learn to rationalize our fears in the same manner as someone we admire, we do tend to think, ''She wouldn't be afraid unless there was a good reason. Whatever her reason may be, it must be good enough for me too.''

As with the other two types of learning we have discussed, association and reward, the seeds of fear must be present in order to learn a fear by imitating someone. By watching others and modeling our behavior on theirs, we cultivate the seeds of fear and make it our own.

In reality, we probably learn our fears through a combination of the three learning processes we have described. More often than not, a number of influences are working in concert when a fear is developed. The important thing is not so much *by what process* the fear was learned, but rather *that it was learned*. For that means that it can also be unlearned.

HOW WE MAINTAIN FEAR

It's not uncommon for people to forget things that they have learned. Foreign languages, card games, and solving algebra problems are all examples of skills that must be practiced and maintained if they are not to be forgotten. It would be nice if the fears we learn could be forgotten so easily. Unfortunately, many of the usual ways that we deal with fears have undesirable side effects. We adopt patterns of behavior that inadvertently serve to maintain and even intensify the very problems we are trying to handle.

If we could *totally* avoid the things we fear with no adverse effects on our lives, then fear would not be much of a problem. But total avoidance is rarely possible. What we typically do instead is to minimize our direct contact with fear-provoking situations by trying to hold them off at some appropriate distance. By keeping a feared situation at some distance away from us—physically, temporally, or emotionally—we attempt to keep the fear from reaching crisis proportions. Often, the methods that we use to achieve these distances actually work against us by keeping our fears alive and strong. Let's see why this is so.

Physical distance can be measured in feet, or yards, or city blocks, or any of a number of other familiar units of measurement. In general, the farther away a feared object is, the less we fear it. A man who is afraid of mice is more afraid of the mouse in his house than of mice in the next county. A person who will take a sixteen-mile detour to avoid crossing a certain bridge is using physical distance to keep fear within manageable bounds.

Barriers such as walls and fences also act as kinds of physical distance. A fenced-in dog may not cause the terror that a loose dog arouses. The familiar confines of an apartment may provide the distance needed to "protect" someone from the imagined fears that lurk beyond.

But notice what actually happens to the person who uses physical distance as a way of holding down fear. A fear-provoking stimulus arises. The person avoids it by getting far enough away from it to reduce the fear. The reduction in fear acts as reinforcement. This is a perfect example of instrumental conditioning or learning by reward. Each time a person puts physical distance between himself and his fear, the pattern of avoidance becomes more firmly entrenched, and the fear continues to get worse.

Temporal distance may be measured in specific units,

such as hours, days, and weeks, or it may be more generally expressed as "some time in the future." Procrastination—putting things off until some unspecified time in the future—allows us to keep temporal distance between ourselves and the things we fear. For people who are afraid to go to the dentist, a dental appointment does not produce much anxiety when it's a month away. As the time gets nearer, however, the fear increases. And if the fear becomes too much, well, we can always postpone it if there's a good enough reason. And there's always a good reason if we really want there to be one. Once again, we are learning by reward. The reduction in fear after telling the dentist, "I can't come in until next month," feels so good that we may just try it again. And again.

Emotional distance is harder to measure than the other two. How close we feel to someone, how much we care about something, what we are willing or unwilling to give up are all measures of emotional distance.

The technique that we use to maintain emotional distance is rationalization. We make up reasons to support what we do. The salesperson who is afraid to fly may rationalize by saying, "Look at all the money I'm saving." The husband who is anxious about being able to have sex, reasons, "She'd probably rather watch television." The woman who is afraid to leave her house says, "I'd rather do things at home than go to those boring choir practices."

A common rationalization is that in which a person says, "I'm afraid to fly because flying is dangerous. Why, just last week I read about a plane crash." This person ignores all the facts that show fewer people are killed in airplanes than in bathtubs.

Maintaining emotional distance from a fear-provoking situation is a particularly insidious form of avoidance. It disguises the real reason why a person behaves a certain way. People who practice these forms of self-deception sometimes have the most difficult time of all in dealing realistically with their fears. They have isolated themselves so thoroughly from the truth that they have difficulty in taking the essential first step in dealing with any problem—admitting that a problem exists. Because self-deception allows us to maintain an emotional distance from the things we fear, it is too often allowed to become part of our behavioral repertoire. As such, it lets us continue to reduce our fear at the expense of other aspects of our lives.

UNLEARNING FEARS

Startle reflexes and a healthy respect for genuinely dangerous situations are the seeds of fears. Whether these seeds grow and assume a dominant role in our lives depends on how we learn to handle the complex emotions, thoughts, and patterns of behavior that we experience as fear. The learning process, which consists of both conscious and unconscious processes, shapes our beliefs so that we expect to be afraid in certain situations, and, thus, we are afraid.

When the seeds of fear begin to take root and grow, there is a strong tendency to adopt patterns of behavior that only make matters worse. We start to avoid the things we fear. As a result, we fail to confront our fears in any constructive way, and they become more intense. We may know that a fear is irrational, that it unduly limits our life, or that it detracts from our pleasure and self-esteem. However, knowledge alone is not enough to let us escape from the power that fear exercises over us.

Fortunately, the processes by which we learn to be afraid can be applied to help us form new patterns of behavior that allow us to cope with fear. We *can learn* to control emotions of fear. We *can learn* to stop thoughts of fear that feed upon themselves and send us spinning out of control. We *can learn* new forms of behavior that enable us to replace tension and anxiety with calmness.

The learning techniques that we have discussed—association, reward, and imitation—can be made to work for us. They will become our tools for learning to fear less.

3.
THE BEHAVIORAL
APPROACH TO FEAR

The techniques that we present for overcoming fear are based on two premises. First, fear is a problem of behavior. Thoughts, emotions, and reactions of the autonomic nervous system may contribute to the problem (and must be dealt with accordingly), but the heart of the problem is behavior. The second premise is that behavior is something we learn through the processes of association, through rewards, and through imitation. This approach is called *behavioral psychology.*

When seen from the viewpoint of behavioral psychology, fear is not the result of some mysterious inner force. Certainly, it is not a form of sickness. Fear, quite simply, is a problem of human behavior, the solution to which is the learning of new forms of behavior. The symptoms of fear and the problems of fear are one and the same. If we get rid of the symptoms, we get rid of the problem. We can treat the symptoms, and hence the problems, by learning new behaviors that replace our fearful response.

OF DEMONS AND DISEASES

In some earlier and more primitive societies, there was a simple explanation for why anyone behaved in any way differently from his fellow human beings. The devil made him do it. The universe abounded with demons ready to jump in and take over any unwary soul. Demons were thought to be the cause of a number of deviations from narrowly defined boundaries. Accordingly, the treatments consisted of persuading the little rascals to vacate the bodies they possessed. This was done by making the body sufficiently uncomfortable that the demon would want to look for more hospitable quarters. Beating the hell out of someone was, quite literally, considered a form of therapy. Sometimes treatments would consist of drilling holes in the patient to expedite the demon's departure. Not surprisingly, a number of patients departed along with the demons.

In the realm of medicine, demons eventually gave way to more tangible causative agents—germs, bacteria, and viruses. The discovery of these tiny organisms, which were hidden from sight without the aid of special instruments, represented a major advance for the practice of medicine.

For the first time, physicians could accurately predict that a person exposed to a certain type of microorganism would develop a particular disease. As a result, people could both change and avoid the conditions and objects that harbored disease-causing agents. New cures for disease could also be developed. Knowing that germs and bacteria caused certain diseases, scientists could create ways of eliminating these organisms and the disease they caused. Medical diagnosis was placed on a far firmer basis than ever before, since physicians could identify a disease by organisms found in the body, and not solely on the basis of physical symptoms, which could vary widely from one individual to the next.

The discovery of microbes as the causes of disease probably contributed as much as any other single factor in placing modern medicine on a firm scientific footing in the diagnosis, prevention, and cure of diseases. The enormous success of medicine in dealing with a disease provided a model of scientific inquiry that was highly regarded and widely imitated in other fields. Sociologists began to look for "hidden causes" that made some societies "sick." Economists turned detective in their search for unseen forces that caused economies to be sick or healthy. One of the most influential extensions of the medical model was in the work of Sigmund Freud, who used the model to create his highly original, incredibly complex, and largely unscientific analysis of human behavior.

FREUD AND THE MEDICAL MODEL OF FEAR

Freud believed that just as there were hidden causes for physical diseases, mental illness also had "invisible" causative agents. He contended that the cause of mental illness was neuroses buried so deeply in the human psyche that they were not normally accessible to our conscious processes of thought and reason. Every so often, neuroses would boil over and spill out in the form of aberrant behavior. The role of psychoanalysis was to guide the patient to a discovery of the hidden causes of the neuroses. By bringing the neuroses out of the dark recesses of the unconscious mind and into the light of consciousness, Freud believed the patient would be cured. Consciousness would allow the patient to cope with the newly uncovered neurosis on a rational basis and would thus remove any need to fall back on irrational forms of behavior.

The application of these techniques to a fear problem is well illustrated in Freud's famous case study of Little Hans, a young boy who developed a strong fear of horses and many objects associated with horses. Little Hans had suffered a traumatic experience one day when he had seen a large horse stumble on a stone and fall. The horse had been going at a fast pace, pulling a heavily loaded cart. The noise and confusion were understandably frightening to the small boy, and he later indicated that he had been afraid the horse might have been killed. Later on, when Hans began to be afraid of horses and carts, and even rocks in the street, his family consulted Dr. Freud.

It is not rational to fear horses and carts, or stones, Freud reasoned, and yet the boy is afraid. Therefore, he must be afraid of something else instead. And whatever that "something else" is, it must be causing the fear.

Applying his psychoanalytic techniques, Freud searched back into Hans' unconscious mind to find the neuroses that caused these irrational fears. The neuroses that Freud looked for generally had to do with such things as feelings about sex, relationships with parents, and early toilet training. Freud believed that these neuroses, which were tucked away in the unconsciousness, somehow managed to attach themselves to symbolic objects in the world. If Little Hans could be made to see the chain of association by which he had attached his neuroses to horses, he would see the irrationality of it all and would thus be cured.

According to Freud, Hans was not *really* afraid of horses and carts; they were only representations of what was *really* bothering him. Freud believed the *real* problem was Hans's concern about his mother's being pregnant. The heavily loaded cart was symbolic of pregnancy, and the spilling of the cart's contents on the street was delivery. The *obvious* similarities, Freud claimed, made it quite natural for Hans to transfer his fear from one to the other. Similarly, Hans wasn't concerned about the horse being killed; it was his father's death that he was afraid of. In addition, Freud noted that heavily loaded horse-drawn carts were quite naturally abhorrent to Hans because he made the "obvious" association with a body heavily loaded with feces and noted the striking resemblance between the manner in which carts pass through gates and feces leave the body.

Freud's psychological theory stirred great interest worldwide, but even its most devoted advocates had to admit to some real problems with it. For one thing, the theory was immensely complex, and it became even more so as practitioners attempted to apply it to new cases. The theory was constantly being stretched, altered, and reinterpreted to fit the facts. Once the theory had been around long enough to gain an air of respectability, practitioners in more than a few cases began to reshape facts to fit the theory.

Another problem with Freudian theory was its reliance on neuroses as hidden causes. It was impossible to inspect neuroses firsthand, since they had no physical reality. They were simply assumptions used to bolster the complex and ingenious theory. Also, there was no clear link between the assumed neuroses and their effects on human behavior. Unlike germs that give rise to a reasonably consistent set of symptoms in physical diseases, neuroses supposedly caused an unlimited variety of widely different effects. Unfortunately for the theory, the connection between supposed causes and effects could not be observed, so there was no way to judge the validity of the theory. In the final analysis, Freudian theory, for all its attempts at scientific methodology, was pretty much a matter of faith; Freud's assumed neuroses were not a great deal more than updated versions of the demons of an earlier time.

BEHAVIORISM AND THE LEARNING MODEL

In the 1920s, the experiments of John B. Watson, a psychology professor at Johns Hopkins University, demonstrated that the behavior of fear could be learned. Watson, who became known as the "Father of Behaviorism," worked with a young boy named Albert to show the relationship of learning to fear. The case is an interesting contrast to the story of Little Hans.

Albert was given a white rat to play with for three weeks. He not only showed no fear of it, but actually was affectionate with it. He would pick up the rat, hold it, and pet it in much the same way a child might play with a doll or a puppy. After three weeks, a new procedure was introduced. When little Albert reached to pick up the rat, a loud startling gong was sounded. The first time this happened, the little boy lost his balance and fell forward on his face. He whimpered, but got back up with no ill effects. The next time he reached for the rat, the noise sounded again. He was visibly startled. Within only a few trials, Albert not only would not reach for the rat, but he also exhibited all the usual symptoms of fear when the animal was put in the pen with him. The technique used to teach him fearful behavior was, of course, classical conditioning or learning by association.

Watson's work was important because it changed the view of fear therapy from a medical model, such as that used by Freud, to a learning model. The learning model was superior in many ways. It involved fewer assumptions, since there was no need to hypothesize hidden causes. It explained the phenomenon directly, rather than indirectly or symbolically as with the Freudian approach. It explained the mechanisms linking causes and effects in a way that could be subjected to scientific inspection and verification.

It is interesting to review the case of Little Hans within the framework of a behavioristic approach. According to Freud's case notes, Hans had at least four experiences in his life when horses had frightened or upset him. So, he had ample opportunity to learn fear by association. In addition, the situational aspects of his fear fit neatly into the learning model. For example, he was more afraid of heavily loaded carts than empty ones, and he was more afraid of large horses than small ones. The intensity of his fears was clearly related to the precise conditions of the traumatic accident involving a large fast-moving horse pulling a heavily loaded cart. Theories are indeed very powerful devices, both for exposing and concealing scientific truth.

The power of behavioral theory did not go unnoticed among practitioners. By the 1950s, several therapists had begun evolving therapeutic approaches based on behavioral learning principles. These therapeutic approaches became collectively known as *behavior therapy*. Perhaps the most notable of these new behavior therapies was the technique designed by Dr. Joseph Wolpe. Dr. Wolpe demonstrated that experimental learning principles could be used to treat fear by gradually exposing a person to the feared situation. He demonstrated that this could be done either in the real world or by using imagined scenes of the feared situation. He called this new technique *systematic desensitization.* Much of what will be described herein is a direct extension of Wolpe's work.

ADVANTAGES OF BEHAVIORAL THERAPY

Experiments have shown that minor variations in a learning situation can result in corresponding variations in human behavior. This accounts for the great differences from one person to another in the way they experience certain fears. For example, the rather common fear of heights is experienced by some people in buildings but not in airplanes. Others are afraid in small airplanes but not in large ones. A person who enjoys flying in an airplane can still be afraid of heights when going over bridges. The things to be feared and the ways of experiencing fears are as varied as the situations in which people learn to be afraid.

Unlike Freudian theory, which searches for the "original causes" of fear, behavioral theory holds that causes are not necessarily relevant to therapy. Therapy does not consist of ferreting out causes, but of creating new learning situations in which new forms of behavior are forged. The Freudian detective work of getting back to childhood's root causes is eliminated, and therapy can proceed at a much faster pace.

Finally, behavior therapy can be successfully conducted on a self-help basis. That is what this book is about. In the following chapters, we will provide the necessary tools for developing learning situations that will let you start changing your behavior.

We start by developing a program that outlines what you hope to achieve in overcoming fears. The program consists of setting specific goals, establishing appropriate levels of expectation at each step along the way, and rewarding your progress in order to reinforce the nonfearful forms of behavior.

We will show you how to rate your fears so that you can judge your progress. We will teach you how to relax, starting in anxiety-free situations and very gradually working closer and closer to the fear-provoking object or situation. You will learn how to stop thoughts of fear. You will learn to control the feelings of fear, even those brought on by the autonomic nervous system. And you will learn to be assertive, both as a means of reducing fear and as a means of avoiding interference with the program you establish to overcome fear.

As you read these next few chapters, keep several points in mind. Your fear is neither silly nor trivial. If you are one of the millions of people who believe that their lives are limited by fear, it is worth the effort to learn new behaviors. With near certainty, your fear springs in part from some earlier form of adaptive behavior; however, if you are honest with yourself, you will admit that your behavior goes well beyond any reasonable effort to avoid actual danger. Consciously or unconsciously, you have fallen victim to learning situations that have nurtured the seeds of fear and thereby affected your life. Through behavioral therapy, either self-administered or in cooperation with a trained practitioner, you can create new learning situations that will allow you to set new expectations about your reactions to fear-provoking situations, that will reduce and eliminate the destructive anxieties generated by fear and that will enhance your own self-image and free you from the limitations that fear places on your life.

4.
LEARNING TO RELAX
AND RELAXING
TO LEARN

Relaxation plays a central role in fear problems for two reasons. First, two sensations that you experience when you are afraid are muscular tension and physiological arousal. By learning to relax, you ease muscle tension, lower your heart rate, increase the flow of saliva to your mouth, and decrease sweating, blood pressure, and respiration rate. In other words, you eliminate many of the unpleasant feelings that you experience as fear.

The second reason is that you learn better and more easily when you are relaxed. Much of learning is a process of the conscious mind. Your conscious mind can handle only a limited number of processes at a time. When you try to go beyond that limit, you make mistakes, grow frustrated, become tense and anxious, and feel that you have no control—all because of the bombardment of stimuli. Anxiety demands that some of your conscious processes be devoted to answering its call—to prepare to fight, or to flee. As a result, when you are anxious, a smaller amount of consciousness is available for learning. Learning is impossible when your consciousness is trying to work beyond its capacity.

Fortunately, the human body can handle a great number of processes without our being consciously aware of them. We breathe, blink our eyes, swallow, maintain our balance while walking, and much more, without having to consciously think about it. Even complex tasks such as driving an automobile become largely automatic.

The consciousness of a person in a state of fear is typically overworked just attending to internal processes. It is busy monitoring how tight the muscles are, how sweaty the hands are, how fast the heart is beating, as well as counting the butterflies in the stomach and worrying whether other people are noticing the fear. So, there is little or no capacity left over to attend to what is happening around you, to practice fear-control techniques—or to do anything else.

The purpose of this chapter is to start you working on relaxation techniques that can be applied in fear-provoking situations. These techniques have a twofold benefit: they help to diminish the feelings of fear, and, at the same time, they free channels of the conscious mind to learn and apply the other new forms of behavior that we suggest for coping with fears.

WHY CAN'T YOU RELAX?

Your muscles and nervous system have a most convenient trait: they adapt readily to varying levels of tension. Through this adaptive ability, your body retains muscular control without your being aware of it. If this were not so, you would spend all your time thinking about the changing state of your muscles. If you sat down to relax, you would find yourself focusing on the muscle tension in your abdomen and buttocks, without which you could not sit upright. If you tried to take a relaxing walk, your conscious mind would be so busy processing information on the forces applied to your muscles and on the required muscular reaction to deal with these forces, that you would very quickly be a nervous wreck.

But, although adaptation lets us function more or less automatically in some situations, it is a mixed blessing. Over a prolonged period of stress, or during shorter periods of severe stress, your body system will adapt to the high levels of muscle tension. You continue to function, often unaware that you are in an abnormally high state of stress. Thus, the feedback signals that normally inform your nervous system to take it easy become unnoticed due to the adaptive process.

Our body systems exhibit another fortunate trait, which, like adaptation, can also work against us if we are not careful. When you exercise your willpower to make your muscles relax, your body does not suddenly go limp and collapse. You probably wouldn't care much for relaxation if you wound up in a crumpled heap on the floor each time you decided to lower your muscle tension. What does happen when you relax is that your muscle tension decreases step by step, a bit at a time. When everything is functioning normally, your nervous system monitors the relaxation process and lets you gradually achieve the level of muscular tension that you desire—not so much that your shoulders ache, but enough that you don't fold up on the floor.

In a fear-provoking situation, we become very tense. The body quickly adapts to this tension, and so we are not even aware of it until it reaches an extremely high level. Only when we become aware of the extreme tension, do we try to do anything about it. Desperately, we try to send our muscles a message to relax. But somehow the message doesn't seem to get through. Frustrated by our inability to control our bodies, we try harder. Yet the harder we try to relax, the more tense we become.

The reason for our inability to relax during such extreme tension is based on a well-known principle of perception, *Weber's law*. The principle is easy to illustrate. Stand in a brightly lit room, and look at a white wall. Now, strike a match. The room is unquestionably brighter, because you just added a new source of light. But the total illumination in the room is so great, and the difference made by adding the light of the match so tiny, that you will notice no change in illumination.

If you lower the lights in the same room, however, you will see quite a different effect when you strike a match. This time you will see the flickering match light up the walls. When the total illumination is low enough, you can easily see the minute change that the match causes.

The application of this principle to relaxation is perfectly straightforward. The greater the tension in our muscles, the less we can sense any easing of that tension. Because our muscles relax in gradual steps, we sometimes cannot notice the change at all if we are very tense. As a result, we are often least able to relax precisely at the times when we most need to.

RELAXATION: A CONSCIOUS COPING STRATEGY

Have you ever seen a man drop a quarter in a vending machine that didn't work? He will first employ some conscious coping strategies to retrieve the quarter. He may press the coin-return lever. He may even jiggle it a few times. If that fails, he may try thumping the front of the machine with a fist on the theory that the coin is lodged and needs to be shaken loose. At this stage, impulse begins to take over quite rapidly. The man may shake the machine, kick it, or curse at it. In fact, a man was once arrested for firing a pistol into a candy machine that had taken his money without giving candy.

As this illustration points out, under stress we regress. Rational, adaptive patterns of behavior give way to more primitive reactions.

Conscious coping strategies are learned, and, in general, they are effective. However, their effective use depends on several factors: you must know that a particular strategy exists, you must know how to employ it properly, and you must recognize when an appropriate situation occurs for employing the strategy.

Relaxation is a coping strategy that can be learned. As with any other learning process, we begin with simple tasks undertaken in optimal conditions and work up to more difficult tasks that can be used in more extreme situations. For only in this way can we call upon the strategy when we most need it.

With sufficient practice, relaxation can become internalized so that usually you will be able to employ it without having to think very hard about it. Relaxation can become an automatic response much as one's actions when driving a car become automatic.

PREPARING TO RELAX

The nervous system of the human body has three divisions: the *central nervous system*, consisting of the brain and spinal chord; the *autonomic nervous system*, which supplies the glands and smooth (sometimes called *involuntary*) muscles; and the *skeletal motor system*, which activates the arms, legs, face, back, and tongue. Fear and stress can cause activity in one or any combination of these three divisions of the nervous system.

The relaxation exercises presented here are designed to relax the skeletal muscles, to quiet the autonomic nervous system, and to focus the brain on a peaceful image that enhances deeper relaxation. As you do the exercises, you may experience some of the following sensations:

- Heaviness of the eyelids.
- Limpness or heaviness of the limbs.
- Slower and deeper breathing. (The diaphragm, a thin sheet of muscle between the abdomen and the lungs, is involved in relaxed breathing.)
- A feeling that events in the world around you are off in the distance somewhere. (Conscious scanning of the outside world diminishes.)
- The heart may seem to beat faster or make a pounding sound. (Body sounds are always present, but they are usually drowned out by our attention to outside events. With deeper relaxation, even body sounds recede from awareness.)
- Hands and feet may become warm, and toes and fingers may become tingly as deep relaxation causes more blood to flow to the extremities.

Since you relax in gradual steps, you may not experience all of these sensations. But if you do feel them, don't be alarmed. You will never relax too deeply too quickly. You may fall asleep though, so you should set an alarm clock.

The relaxation technique presented here requires that you focus your attention on the way your muscles feel when they are tense and, by contrast, how they feel when they are relaxed. The technique requires that you consciously tense certain muscle groups and consciously relax them, and that you learn to associate the word *relax* with this process. The word association will serve to cue your relaxation response in fear-provoking situations. With repetition, you can learn the patterns of smooth, concentrated tension applied to each muscle group and the progressively deeper relaxation that occurs upon release of that tension.

USING A TAPE RECORDER

You can buy a small portable tape recorder for less than thirty dollars, and it will benefit you in learning to relax. By recording the instructions for the exercises presented here, you can then carry them out without having to worry about the sequence of instructions. This in effect frees one of the channels of your consciousness, which can then be devoted to the learning process. The recorded instructions let you concentrate on what you are doing without your having to check constantly to see if you are doing it right.

Recording the instructions yourself may be helpful in learning to talk to yourself. Remember, you are trying to learn to relax as a *conscious* coping strategy. This requires that you say to yourself from time to time, "Hey self, you're starting to tense up. Better relax. That's it, just slow down and relax." Hearing your own voice in relaxation exercises reinforces your ability to talk down your fear when the need arises.

One word of caution about the tape recorder. Read the instructions *very* slowly; otherwise, you'll later become tense just trying to keep up. Also, read in a calm, even voice. Don't worry if you don't sound like a professional announcer.

PROGRESSIVE MUSCLE RELAXATION

To practice progressive muscle relaxation, go into a quiet room and get into a comfortable position—sit in a chair, lie on the floor, get into whatever position is best for you. If you can dress comfortably, without tight-fitting clothes, it will be easier for you to relax—loosen your tie, slip off your girdle. Choose a time when you won't be interrupted. Depending on where you are, you might want your secretary to intercept visitors for half an hour, or you might want to take the phone off the hook or send the kids out to play. After you have recorded the following exercise on tape, just play it back and follow the instructions. Don't be put off by the apparent simplicity of the exercise. Try it.

BEGIN RECORDING HERE. READ SLOWLY. AT EACH DASH, PAUSE 1 SECOND.

Let your eyes drift shut---and settle down as best you can.--- For the next few moments, begin to adopt an attitude--that nothing is of much importance other than concentrating on this exercise and relaxing.------Begin by directing your internal attention to the feet. Slowly, begin to bend both your feet at the ankles---bending the feet upward so that the toes arc upward toward the knees---building the tension slowly so that you can study it as it builds in the area where you lace your shoes---in the shins---and in the calves.--Build it slowly under your control---up to a point, equally in both feet, where they neither shake nor hurt.---You are controlling the tension in that part of your body, building it under your control to a level of rock-solid tension now.------Hold it there, study it, and when you are ready---think the word RELAX, and slowly let the tension go.---Study the relaxation as it comes into those muscles under your control, pleasantly deeper---and--deeper under your control. Smoothly allowing your feet to achieve their most comfortable position.--Letting the relaxed muscles find that position without your stretching them in the opposite direction.--That's good.--

Now focus your attention on the muscles of the thighs.--- Imagine that your two relaxed feet are heavy weights.-----

Begin to make a motion to lift your lower legs from the knees.----Try not to bend your feet.---Keep the legs, from the knees down, as one unit. Slowly make the motion as if you were lifting.----Concentrate on the tension building in the thighs under your control.--Build the tension without actually lifting the heels---hold it there---study the tension.---Now think RELAX.--Slowly letting the tension go--study the relaxation as it flows into your legs under your control---deeper--and deeper--that's good. As your legs continue to relax, the legs will tend to roll outward with the feet tending to spread, rolling on the heels.---As your legs continue to relax--deeper and deeper--focus your attention on the buttocks.---Begin to tense them by pinching them together and folding them upward and inward-----rolling your relaxed legs even further outward as you build the tension under your control. It's as if you were sitting on a block of concrete getting more and more solid.---Feel yourself being lifted by the increasing tension under your control.--Build the tension up to maximum now, to a point where they neither shake nor hurt.----Hold it there.--Now think the word RELAX, and let the tension go.--Feel the relaxation coming into those muscles under your control--as if you were sinking into a soft cushion, pleasantly deeper--and deeper.--That's right.--Try to follow the flow of relaxation just a little deeper.---------

Now focus your attention on your abdomen.---Begin to tense this sheet of muscle by slowly pulling the navel inward toward the backbone. Breathe---more and more with the upper part of the chest. Building the tension under your control. Continue breathing with the upper half of your chest, and notice that you can breathe regardless of where tension is in your body. Hold the tension at maximum now, and think RELAX, letting the abdomen sag, relaxing more and more under your control.---It doesn't matter what you look like when you relax, what is important is that you are relaxing deeper and deeper. Notice that your breathing moves downward as this muscle relaxes---abdominal breathing is relaxed breathing---that's good.----------

Now direct your internal attention to the hands.---Begin to build the tension in both hands equally by arching the fingertips and hands upward and backward, bending at the wrist, back toward the elbow. Building the tension under your control in the back of the hand and in the forearms---slowly up to the point where they neither shake nor hurt--hold that tension at maximum now; you are in control--study it.--Now think RELAX, and slowly let the tension go.--Study the relaxation as it flows--deeper and deeper under your control---you are relaxing your hands and arms, deeper and deeper. Allow the sensation of relaxation to flow to the rest of the muscles of your body---let the chair [or bed] support your body---relaxing.------Now concentrate on the muscles in the back of the neck and the shoulders.---Begin by slowly raising the shoulders---upward and slightly backward---letting your arms roll outward.---At the same time, begin to tilt your head *slowly* backward, building the tension in the back of the neck and right between the shoulders. Breathe---it is very important that you breathe during this exercise.--Continue with gently building the tension as if you were going to stuff your shoulders into your ears.----DO NOT FORCE THIS EXER-CISE. The slow gentle building of tension to a point where there is no shaking or discomfort is what is important. Allow your mouth to open, breathe as if you were breathing through a straight pipe---upward. Hold the tension, now RELAX--let the tension go. Feel the relaxation flow outward along the shoulders as they sag--allow your head to gently tilt forward.--Feel the relaxation up the back of your neck--spreading out over your back--relaxing--deeper and deeper. Your shoulders are drooping more and more, your head---tilting forward more and more--relaxing. As your head comes forward, let it rest in whatever position is most comfortable.---Relaxing.------Now focus your attention on your forehead.--With your eyes still closed, begin to raise your eyebrows, wrinkling your forehead.--You are building the tension in that part of your body under your control. Slowly, build it up to maximum-----hold it there---study it---now think RELAX, and slowly let the relaxation flow--like a piece of rumpled silk smoothing, smoothing--over the top of your head and down over the upper part of your face--smoother--and smoother.---Now the muscles of the eyelids and the muscles around the eyes.slowly and gently shut your eyes tighter and tighter without excessive force, building the tension smoothly up to that point of maximum, then hold it there.--Study the tension under your control---then--RELAX--letting the tension go---relaxing and feeling the relaxation deeper and deeper--as if the relaxation is dissolving the tension around the eyes.----

Now begin to drive the corners of the mouth deeper and deeper into the cheeks--building the tension in a tight smile-- slowly up to a point of maximum tension.--Each time you repeat the exercise this maneuver will become smoother and smoother under your control. Hold it at maximum.---Now RELAX, studying the relaxation as it flows into the cheeks under your control.--As it flows, your lips slowly part--your jaw sags---relaxing deeper and deeper. Your tongue resting.--- Continue relaxing for a moment or two.---------Enjoy the pleasant feelings in your body, which you have allowed under your own control--------------.

Now without force begin a slow deepening breath all the way into a comfortable depth--slow, unhurried, and smooth.-- The air is flowing in; you are getting all the air you need. There should be no force or jerkiness to the flowing. Hold it and think RELAX--letting the air flow like air coming out of a balloon.--Let the air do the work, not the muscles.--Feel the pleasant, easy settling in your chest--relaxing deeper and deeper--then let your body breathe for you at its own pace. At night when you sleep, your body breathes perfectly for the needs of your body--slowly, easily. Your body knows how to breathe for its own needs better than you do--so let it do so, and imagine the following scene. You are sitting in a comfortable lounge chair out in nature.---Before you is a small, green field covered with lush grass.--It is neither too hot nor too cold.---The sounds of the city are off in the distance somewhere.---In the middle of the field is a tall, strong tree covered with broad green leaves. From where you sit, you can see the tree comfortably.---At the very top of the tree, notice that one leaf becomes detached---and begins to drift--from side--to side--drifting, settling effortlessly---so softly--so gently--that when it finally comes to rest---it will hardly bend a single blade of grass.--Picture the leaf drifting, floating from side--- to side---soon coming to rest---as you are in the scene--- calming---resting---deeper and deeper under your control.---- Allow the leaf to come to rest now---relaxing---. Picture it resting there---without effort, its own gentle weight supported by the grass---without the slightest bit of effort---an effortless balance---just like your body supported by the chair---effortlessly.----

Enjoy the deep calm you are providing yourself.----Each time you do this exercise you become more and more familiar with the pattern of relaxation in your body.---Your concentration becomes stronger---concentrating on the elements of the exercise that allow the pattern of relaxation to emerge more and more.-------------When you feel ready, begin to think of reorienting to the room.--From time to time a feeling of wanting to stretch will come to your muscles.---Allow that feeling to occur.---Notice how freely the breath moves in your lungs.---Soon your eyelids will begin to flutter---allow them to--getting lighter and lighter---as if they want to open on their own.---Any weight that was there dissolves.---When they open, your eyes will be crystal clear, your senses crisp. As your eyes begin to open, notice that your body can be at ease and your mind active. Enjoy the benefits of relaxation you have provided yourself.---You can marshal your body for the tasks at hand any time you wish--but for a moment or two, reorient to the room, and enjoy the calm under your control.

TIPS ON PRACTICING RELAXATION

Start fresh. Too often, people associate relaxation with fatigue. The experience of the two is somewhat similar; however, they should not be confused. When you are relaxed, your mind is active. You remain alert. You are able to think clearly and learn quickly. With fatigue, on the other hand, the mind is dull and inactive. It is difficult to take in new information, and you may tend to doze off.

Be sure to practice relaxing when you are not tired. Remember, practicing relaxation is not goofing off. On the contrary, it is learning one of the most valuable of all techniques for controlling fear. You learn better when you are fresh. Blanking out in front of a television set or going to sleep at the end of a tiring day does not teach you anything about relaxing.

Preliminaries. If you are especially tense, you may need to do more than settle down in a quiet spot for a few minutes during the day. Some people find that a warm bath helps them to calm down enough so that they can concentrate fully on relaxation exercises. Warm milk is another preliminary that some people find useful. Others start by listening to music.

As explained earlier, tension creates a vicious circle. The more tense you get, the harder it becomes to relax. Thus, if you begin the exercises by lowering the background levels of stress, you will find it easier to practice the progressive relaxation techniques and guided imagery. You will be learning to relax and relaxing to learn.

Go **S-L-O-W-L-Y.** Whatever you do, don't be in a hurry to get through your relaxation exercises. Nothing is more self-defeating than putting yourself under artificial time restraints.

Sometimes, people find the exercises are not working as well as they might like. So they simply try harder. Of course, that just makes matters worse—you relax by getting rid of pressures, not by adding to them. Relaxation is a process of letting go and learning to trust your body. Fearful people try to force control, which in itself may increase anxieties. Take it easy, and don't try too hard.

USING PRERECORDED TAPES

Although you can make a perfectly adequate tape for these exercises yourself, you may want to buy a prerecorded tape of relaxation methods just for some variety. In addition, some people simply don't like the sound of their own voice. If you don't, use a prerecorded tape or have a friend tape the exercise for you. Prerecorded tapes are available from the organization listed at the end of this chapter.

SOME OTHER RELAXATION TECHNIQUES

In this chapter, we have focused on only two types of relaxation exercises—deep-muscle relaxation and guided imagery. There are many variations on these basics, some of which have been very highly developed. It is interesting to note that virtually all relaxation techniques share common features with those we have described here.

For instance, one of the best-known relaxation techniques is the *body massage.* Like progressive relaxation, a massage typically covers the same major muscle groups. In progressive relaxation, you stretch the muscles and command them to relax, whereas, in a massage, the tensing effort is exerted by another person. The principles are the same. However, massage is not a substitute for the progressive techniques that you should learn and carry out on your own.

Meditation is essentially a form of guided imagery. Instead of focusing on a tranquil scene, however, the meditator concentrates on a pleasant sound (sometimes called a *mantra*). Religious ceremonies often make use of guided imagery techniques, as in prayer. Eastern religions in particular incorporate relaxation techniques into their rituals: pleasant sounds, pleasant images, a quiet place. However, meditation cannot be accomplished while you are focusing attention on other things. Therefore, it is not an appropriate technique to use in dealing with fear.

If you find these techniques pleasant or useful, by all means take advantage of them. Be aware, however, that these practices are directed at goals other than just conquering fear. Because the goals are broader and less specific, the techniques may be less efficient than the progressive relaxation and guided imagery techniques we have supplied.

In recent years, a great deal of attention has been given to a new relaxation technique called *electromyograph biofeedback*. This procedure requires the use of very sensitive and sophisticated electronic equipment. The equipment senses minute changes in muscular tension or in activities of the autonomic nervous system. These changes are signaled by a flashing light, beeping tone, or some other observable cue. In theory, a person should be able to develop improved relaxation responses by being informed, via the feedback signal, of when small decreases of tension occur. Electromyograph biofeedback must be administered by a qualified practitioner with appropriate equipment.

Finally, we should say a few words about drugs and alcohol as relaxants. Both have undesirable side effects. Both have a potential for abuse that can far outweigh the relatively brief relief they offer. In addition, both can serve to make fears worse by lessening self-control.

Nevertheless, in some cases, drugs play a vital role by providing a temporary tranquilizing effect that allows severely disturbed persons to achieve sufficient control over unconscious processes so that conscious processes begin to take effect once again. Used in this way and taken under adequate supervision, drugs have a place. They are not, however, a substitute for learning to cope.

Additional Information

Relaxation tapes may be purchased for $9.95 postpaid from Behavior Modification Associates, 25 Huntington Avene, Boston, Massachusetts 02116.

Anxiety and Tension Control: A Physiologic Approach, Edmund Jacobson, Lippincott, 1964.

5.
CUTTING FEAR DOWN TO SIZE

This chapter is about goals—about setting and achieving them. One of the most common mistakes people make when trying to conquer a fear is to set unrealistic goals for themselves. They try to do too much too fast. And as a result, they fail. Their thoughts, emotions, and bodily responses overpower their will to be unafraid. The frightened child tells herself, "It's a nice dog. I know it won't hurt me. I'll make myself pet the dog, just reach out, and . . . ." At the last second, she pulls her hand away and backs off, her heart pounding with fear.

A man afraid to speak before a group says, "I know I'm just being silly. There's nothing to be afraid of. I'll make myself go out there, and then I'll be alright." But when he gets in front of the group, he freezes.

A woman who is afraid to ride the subway forces herself to get on anyway. As the doors close and the subway moves out of the station, she bites her lip and clutches her seat. Trembling and panic-stricken, she gets off at the first stop, feeling foolish and very much a failure.

Each time we fail to overcome fear, the fear grows

stronger. Therefore, it is of the utmost importance that we break the failure habit and begin to develop expectations of success. This can only be done by starting with goals that we know we can achieve. We will start to shape new patterns of behavior in easy situations and gradually build up to the harder ones, using each success as a stepping stone to a new goal.

In this chapter, we introduce the first step in a three-step process called *systematic desensitization.* First, you must establish goals that let you gradually move closer to your fears. (Remember, *closer* means decreasing the spatial, temporal, or emotional distance that we discussed in Chapter 2.) The second step is to learn to relax. The third step is to apply relaxation techniques as you move closer to your fears. We start by presenting some basic guidelines for setting realistic goals and arranging these goals in order of increasing difficulty.

STARTING WITH FUNDAMENTALS

When we learn to do something new—play tennis, sail a boat, or drive a car, for example—we do not just learn a *single* new thing, but many.

Consider the familiar example of learning to drive a car. We first learn some facts about automobiles—that the brake pedal is to the left of the gas pedal, that the drive gear lets us go forward, and so on. We also learn how to do certain things—to steer, signal, and brake. The learning process involves remembering these facts and practicing certain simple skills, until they become second nature, so that we can put them all together without even thinking about them.

Virtually everything we do is a complex skill involving knowledge of basic facts about the world, about the particular task we want to accomplish, and about ourselves.

Learning to do something requires that we become adept at combining a number of relatively simple physical and mental skills in order to accomplish our goals. As children, we learn first to crawl, later to pull up to a standing position, to balance and take a few faltering steps, and eventually to walk, skip, and run.

Athletic coaches stress the need for their athletes to "keep going back to fundamentals," that is, practicing the simple tasks that go together to make up the complex moves and strategies of their sport. Failure to recognize the complex nature of an activity and to master fundamentals is very often at the root of one's being unable to perform that activity.

It is particularly important for people with fear problems to understand the complexity of a task. Riding a subway, going to the dentist, and flying in an airplane are all complex tasks, which consist of many different parts and are every bit as varied as skiing, sailing, or playing football. The person who says, "I know how to ride a subway, but I'm afraid," is like the person who says, "I know how to ride a horse, but I keep falling off." Being able to perform a task means that you can perform it at some recognizable level of competence, below which we can safely say that you don't *really* know how to do it. Thus, a person who cannot ride the subway without feeling panic does not really know how to ride the subway. Some parts of the task have not been mastered, and only a return to fundamentals will help.

REJECTING THE ALL-OR-NOTHING APPROACH

Liz M. works as a market researcher in Boston. She is afraid to ride the subway, and her fear puts severe restraints on her life. She usually rides to work with a friend who drives a car. If her friend is not going into Boston, Liz can still get to work by a combination of long walks and changing buses several times. When it rains or snows and Liz's friend does not drive in, she either has to spend twelve dollars for a taxi or call in sick.

Getting home in the evening can also be a problem for Liz. Several times when her evening ride did not show up, she stayed in a hotel in Boston rather than take the subway home. Her social life is affected too, because she can't see her office friends after work unless she can arrange to get home without having to take the subway.

Liz recognizes that her fear is irrational. She has tried several times to "just grit her teeth and brave it out," but her fear is too strong. Once when she forced herself to get on the subway, her fear caused her to get off several stops before her office and to walk the rest of the way. Another time she managed to get on, but then had to leave at the very first stop. Several times, she has paid the fare and then backed out at the last moment. These experiences have left her badly shaken, and they have greatly lowered her self-esteem and confidence. Because she has tried and failed several times, she simply says, "I'm too afraid. I just can't handle it, so I don't try any more."

Liz is taking an "all-or-nothing" approach to her problem. She believes that she either must be able to ride the subway all the way to work during peak rush hours, or else not ride it at all. She sees no middle ground. As a result, when she tries to confront her problem, she does so under the worst possible circumstances.

Let's look at the reasons that Liz's well-intentioned efforts are almost sure to fail.

1. She tries to ride during rush hour when the crowds and confusion are at their worst. She is overloaded with stimuli. Also, her fears about subway riding are made worse by unrelated anxiety about getting to work on time and being able to work after a frightening ride on the subway.

2. The stimulus overload and her concern about getting

to work mean that Liz cannot concentrate on controlling her fear. She has chosen to confront her fear in the situation that has the least chance for success.

3. Each time she tries to overcome her fear, she starts in the very situation where her history of failure is strongest— namely, getting to work during rush hour. Experience has taught her that failure is likely, and her expectations are that she may well fail again.

In coping with fear, we must start by totally discarding the all-or-nothing approach. This can be done if we understand that any task can be broken into simpler tasks. These simpler tasks usually involve either no fear at all, or greatly reduced levels of fear. We can usually learn to carry out these tasks fairly easily. In so doing, our confidence grows, and we can begin to put these subtasks together. We build up gradually, step by step, to the point of being able to carry out the whole task that we have set as a goal.

If we continue to practice the fundamentals that we have built up in our program, the fear will become less and less. The more often we face up to the situations that we fear, the less we will come to fear them. When we are able to stop avoiding the things we fear, we learn that we are masters of the situation and that we are in control, and gradually the fear subsides.

LEARNING BY STEPS

Let's contrast Liz's all-or-nothing approach with a well-planned learning program. Sailing offers a good example. As a would-be sailor, you probably start out on dry land— watching others sail, talking to people who sail and perhaps reading books on sailing. You wait for a good day with just the right amount of breeze, and you choose a calm lake or sheltered inlet for your first attempt. You may begin by just sitting in the boat while it is still at the dock, getting the feel of things, learning where things are. Unless you are particularly adventurous, you probably bring along an instructor, perhaps a friend who sails. Maybe at first you just watch your friend sail, and then you take over the tiller while your friend handles the sails. After a while, you handle the sails, and your friend tillers. Finally, you put it all together, and you are on your way to becoming a sailor. You aren't yet ready to maneuver the boat in a tricky wind, and you can't navigate by the stars, but you have begun to acquire the basic skills of sailing.

Let's focus on the important points of this example:

1. Before you ever went sailing, you familiarized yourself with important aspects of it, so you had some idea of what to expect.

2. You did not attempt the entire job at once. You broke the task into smaller parts, each of which you mastered separately before trying to put them together.

3. You selected the best possible conditions for your first lesson, thereby greatly increasing your chances of success.

4. You worked up gradually to develop the range of skills needed to handle more difficult tasks under less than ideal conditions.

These are the same features that we will apply in learning to cope with a fearful situation.

IDENTIFYING YOUR FEARS

To begin, you will need a quiet room where you can sit and concentrate for a period of time without being disturbed. The room should have a place where you can sit and write comfortably. You will need a stack of 3-by-5-inch index cards and a pencil.

Start by writing down the fear that you want to overcome.

For people who have a single specific fear that they want to work on, this is quite simple. If you have several fears and are not certain which one you want to concentrate on first, make a list. Write down all your fears. Don't think that any one of them is too silly or trivial to include. Study the list, and look for common features, such as fears that involve heights, closed spaces, dark places, being alone, being with many people, going to the doctor or dentist, taking an exam, and so on. In all probability, you will find that most of your fears can be classified into a few of these broader groups. By grouping your fears in this way, you have already made substantial progress. You have narrowed the field in such a way that you can begin to focus on a single group.

Don't try to tackle all the groups at once. Pick one. If there is one group, or a single fear, that you think will be easier to work with, start with that one. It really doesn't matter which one you pick. The important thing is to start with one. People sometimes discover an unexpected side effect when they begin to conquer fear; they discover that their self-esteem starts to rise and that other fears begin to diminish, even though no conscious effort has gone into dealing with them. This generalizing effect may work for you, but don't be disappointed if it doesn't. Just concentrate on overcoming one fear at a time. That way you are most likely to achieve your goal. Anything beyond that should be considered a bonus.

Just one word of caution. Sometimes people can't put their finger on precisely what they are afraid of. They find themselves frightened and anxious in a wide range of apparently unrelated situations. If this happens to you after you have practiced the exercises outlined in Chapter 4, you may want to consider seeking help from a professional therapist who can look at the problem objectively.

DIVIDING YOUR FEAR INTO PIECES

Having selected a specific fear to work on, the next step is to understand the complexity of the situation. You can then begin to break it into smaller pieces, which make it easier to learn to handle.

1. Look at the first card on which you have defined the fear you want to overcome. Now, on another card, describe very briefly a scene in which you would experience that fear to the fullest. For example, if you wrote down "fear of cats," your description of a most fearful scene might be "holding a full-grown male cat in my lap." The following examples illustrate other scences.

Fear	Most Fearful Scene
I am afraid to go to the dentist.	Sitting in a dentist's chair, having a tooth drilled.
I am afraid of public speaking.	Delivering an unprepared talk to a roomful of people I don't know.
I am afraid of riding subways.	Riding the subway to work during the peak rush hour.

2. Write a description of a scene that involves some aspect of your fear, but does not frighten you. You may have to dig pretty deep to come up with something, but you can do it. Think in terms of being separated from the actual situation by distance or time, or else pick some very small aspect of the actual situation. You may feel that any situation involving your fear, however remotely, contains some element of anxiety for you. But if you think hard enough, you can come up with something. You may be afraid of all cats, but what about a picture of a cat? If the picture provokes fear, think in terms of a cat locked up in a

cage in the next room. If that's too close for comfort, think about a cat on the moon. If that's the closest you can get without feeling fear, write it down on the index card. The examples that follow illustrate other nonfearful scenes.

Fear	*Least Fearful Scene*
I am afraid to go to the dentist.	Making a dental appointment six months in advance.
I am afraid of public speaking.	Saying good morning to a casual acquaintance at the office.
I am afraid of riding the subway.	Walking past the subway entrance without any intention of getting on.

3. You have described a most fearful and a least fearful scene. Now, describe as many "in-between cases" as you can think of. You should be able to come up with at least six to eight scenes on your own. If you are exceptionally creative and can think of hundreds of variations, you may want to stop at around twenty or thirty.

This third step is the tricky part. It is also the most important. So here are some guidelines to help you out.

● Imagine yourself getting ready to go into the fear-provoking situation, then going into it, then being in it. At each of these steps, you should be able to describe one or more "in-between" scenes.

● As you describe the scenes, be specific. Think about what you do with your hands, your feet, and your whole body when you are in the situation. Try to be aware of what thoughts are going through your mind when you are experiencing the fear. What is the environment around you? How does it smell, what do you see, what noises do you hear? These specifics will provide valuable clues as to the best way of developing your self-help program.

● Remember what we said in Chapter 2 about fear and distance. The closer we get to a feared situation, either physically or in time, the greater the fear. One way of describing in-between scenes is to vary the distance from the feared situation. You can start with the least feared situation and describe scenes that lead you closer to the most feared scene. In the examples that follow, the fear of cats illustrates decreasing *physical* distance. Fear of going to the dentist illustrates decreasing *temporal* distance.

● A great many more fears are related to specific situations than to specific objects. Describing in-between scenes for these fears involves varying the situation in such a way that we vary the anxiety that we feel. The examples given for fear of public speaking and riding the subway illustrate ways of varying situational types of fears.

● Imagination plays a large role in fear problems. As you describe fearful scenes, you may find yourself growing fearful and anxious just because you are thinking about your fear. This is perfectly normal. If it happens, just get up and walk away from the task. Don't feel that you have to make your complete list in one sitting. If you can, that's fine. If not, take your time.

Example 1. Fear of Cats*

1. Holding a full-grown male cat in my lap.
2. Holding a kitten in my lap.
3. Touching a full-grown cat.

---

*In Examples 1 through 4, the situations are listed in order of most fearful to least fearful.

4. Touching a kitten.
5. Going into a room with a cat in it.
6. Being in the same house with a cat.
7. Seeing a real cat outdoors, from a distance.
8. Seeing a picture of a cat.
9. Thinking of a cat roaming free.
10. Thinking of a cat in a cage.

In this example, physical distance is the primary variable; that is, the closer the cat, the greater the fear. Note, however, that the example includes such situational variables as large cats versus kittens, real cats versus imaginary ones, and free-roaming versus constrained cats.

Example 2. Fear of Going to the Dentist

1. Sitting in the dentist's chair having your teeth drilled.
2. Sitting in the dentist's chair waiting to have your teeth drilled.
3. Sitting in the dentist's waiting room.
4. Walking into the dentist's office.
5. Standing in front of the building where the dentist's office is.
6. Driving to the dentist's office.
7. Waking up in the morning and realizing that today is the day to go to the dentist.
8. Going to the dentist.
9. Thinking about going to the dentist the day before you go.
10. Thinking about going to the dentist a week before you go.
11. Thinking about going to the dentist a month before you go.
12. Making an appointment to go to the dentist six months in advance.

In this example, temporal distance is the main variable. As the actual event gets closer in time, the fear grows.

Example 3. Fear of Public Speaking

1. Delivering an unprepared talk to a large roomful of people I don't know.
2. Reading from a prepared statement to a roomful of people I don't know.
3. Reading from a prepared statement to a small group of people I don't know.
4. Answering questions before a small group of people I don't know.
5. Being a participant in a meeting of fewer than six people whom I know only slightly.
6. Being a participant in a meeting of three people whom I know only slightly.
7. Meeting with three friends to discuss business.
8. Talking with a group of more than three friends at a cocktail party.
9. Talking with two business associates in my office.
10. Greeting a casual acquaintance at the office.

This is an example of situational fear. The fear is varied by the intensity of the stimulus—by the number of people involved, how well they are known, the type of discussion involved, and whether the speaker has a prepared statement or is just talking off the cuff.

Example 4. Fear of Riding the Subway

1. Riding the subway to work during peak rush hours.
2. Riding to work with a friend during rush hour.
3. Riding to work alone during off-peak hours.
4. Riding to work with a friend during off-peak hours.

5. Riding alone from one stop to the next, then getting off.
6. Riding with a friend from one stop to the next, then getting off.
7. Getting on the subway and getting right off before it leaves.
8. Standing in the subway station watching the trains go past.
9. Walking down the stairs into the subway station.
10. Walking up to the subway entrance and not going in.
11. Walking past the subway entrance with no intention of going in.

In this example, the fear varies with such situational elements as independence (riding alone or with a friend) and additional stimuli (large crowds versus no crowds); the fear also varies with distance variables (such as walking past, going downstairs).

RANKING YOUR FEARS

When you have described a number of fear situations on the index cards, the next task is to arrange the cards in order from the least fearful to the most. This is not as difficult as it might seem.

We can rank fears according to the *SUD scale. SUD* stands for *subjective units of discomfort.* The scale goes from 0 to 100. A rating of 0 means that the situation does not excite any fear. Assign a 0 rating to the least fearful situation, and write it on the card. A rating of 100 on the SUD scale is assigned to the most fearful situation and noted on the appropriate card.

Now take the other cards, and assign them a SUD rating somewhere between 0 and 100, according to the intensity of the fear that they arouse in you. The numbers are completely arbitrary. They have absolutely no meaning beyond your own personal experience. They are simply a useful way of helping you arrange the cards in order.

When you have assigned SUD numbers to each situation, lay the cards in front of you and observe how the numbers run. Ideally, the numbers should show a reasonably even spread from 0 to 100, with no two items being more than 10 SUD points apart. If the numbers are crowded near the top or bottom, think of other situations that fall in between and add some additional scenes.

To illustrate, look back at Example 1. The person who drew this up did not originally include item 2. However, touching a full-grown cat (item 3) had a rating of 80 SUD points, which meant a jump of 20 points up to item 1. After some thought, the person decided that holding a small kitten would not be as bad as holding a full-grown cat. That scene was added and assigned a rating of 90 to give an even spread.

The ranking of fears will be the determining factor in how you set up your learning program. You will start at the very bottom and work your way up, gradually, step by step. Be aware that the scenes as you have described them and arranged them in order from 0 to 100 form a *stimulus hierarchy*. You start from stimuli that do not provoke fear and gradually work your way up through the hierarchy to stimuli that provoke increasing amounts of fear.*

Just as fears and the precise way that they are experienced may vary greatly from one person to the next, so stimulus hierarchies will be quite different for each person. If you have any of the common fears that we have shown in our

---

*You should be able to experience a SUD rating of 0 to 10 for the least fearful scene after practicing the relaxation exercises outlined in Chapter 4. If you cannot reach that low a level after practicing these exercises for at least three weeks, you may want to seek professional assistance.

examples, don't be surprised if your stimulus hierarchy turns out quite differently. One of the strengths of the behavioral approach to fear is the ability to adjust to individual differences. Just as people have learned their fears in all different ways, they must be prepared to unlearn and reshape their responses in a variety of ways.

These cards that you have prepared will be your stepping stones to overcoming your fear. Be ready to add cards as you go along. Stepping stones don't serve their purpose if they are so far apart that you can't step easily from one to the next. Thus, you must be flexible enough to recognize when there are gaps in your program and to add new situations that allow you to progress upward through your stimulus hierarchy.

Additional Information

Behavior Therapy Techniques, Joseph Wolpe, Pergamon Press, 1966.
Self-Directed Systematic Desensitization, W.W Wenrich, H.H. Dawley, and D.A. General, Behaviordelia, 1976.

6.
SYSTEMATIC DESENSITIZATION

In Chapter 5, we introduced the concept of fear hierarchies—descriptions of scenes that arouse varying degrees of fear in you as measured by subjective units of discomfort (SUD). Before you begin to carry out the steps in this chapter, you should have constructed your own hierarchy for the fear you will be trying to overcome. Make sure that the scenes are described in some detail, and arrange the 3-by-5-inch index cards in order from the lowest SUD rating to the highest.

In Chapter 4, you began to learn how to relax. You should be well in control of those relaxation techniques, before you begin systematic desensitization. In addition, you should be able to lower your SUD rating to no more than 0 to 10 points in a completely peaceful, nonstressful situation.

In this chapter, you will start to put everything together. As you work through the procedures herein, you will be moving closer and closer to your fear. You must not skip steps. You must not go too fast. The effectiveness of systematic desensitization depends upon your moving at a pace that is completely comfortable for you at all times. You don't want to change your avoidance behavior all at once—you want to change it gradually, systematically. Therefore, you will learn to confront your fear a piece at a time.

Let us begin by considering how and why systematic desensitization works. An understanding of the principles that underlie the exercises can have two important benefits for you. First, it should help you to make the most effective use of the techniques in your particular situation. Second, it should enable you to enter the program with a much more positive commitment toward making the techniques work for you.

HOW SYSTEMATIC DESENSITIZATION WORKS

A fearful situation evokes a number of bodily responses, such as muscular tension, sweating, an increase in heart rate and respiration, and other symptoms. The purpose of systematic desensitization is to replace these fearful responses with relaxation responses. To accomplish this, we will take full advantage of the three types of learning that we discussed earlier. First, you will use *learning by association* to link relaxation with the scenes depicted in your fear hierarchy. Second, through a carefully constructed program that provides reinforcement for your progress, you will be learning through rewards. Third, you will imitate nonfearful behaviors as you begin learning to confront your fear in actual situations.

The first step in systematic desensitization is to defuse a wide range of images and words that you have come to associate with your fears. When we imagine a fearful situation, our bodily responses are often almost as strong as if we actually were in the real situation. Indeed, it is our imagination that works most strongly to keep us from being able to confront our fears. In nearly all instances of fearful behavior, the *imagined* consequences of the fear far exceed any harm that the person has actually experienced. For that reason, it is important to attack fear first at the level of our imagination.

We can do this by working through the cards in our fear hierarchy and learning to substitute relaxation responses for fearful responses *in imaginary situations only*. Approached in this way, the powerful force that imagination exercises over us in fear is made to work in our favor. For, in learning to relax in an imagined situation, we have also taken a giant step toward being able to relax in a real situation. Only when you have completely mastered the ability to relax while *imagining* a fearful situation, however, should you attempt to confront the *real* situation.

Figure 6-1 makes clear the effect at work in systematic desensitization. The numbers on the left of the figure represent the degree of fear as measured on the SUD scale by an individual. The items in the fear hierarchy are listed along the bottom of the chart. Starting with item 1, the

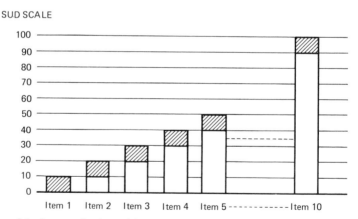

Figure 6-1. Systematic desensitization shifts the threshold of fear so you enter each new step at a lower level of arousal.

individual practices imagining that scene and applying relaxation techniques.

When item 1 draws no more than a point or two on the SUD scale, the person goes on to step 2.* At this step, the goal is to lower the response by 20 points. However, 10 points have already been achieved toward this goal, leaving only another 10 to go. For each item in the hierarchy, the individual practices relaxation techniques until that item draws 0 to 10 on the SUD scale. By the time an individual works up to the final step, it will be possible to lower the SUD rating by a full 100 points. But note that 90 points will have already been achieved toward that goal in the previous steps. At no step is the person ever trying to overcome more than 10 points at a time.

What is actually being accomplished as you work your way through a desensitization program is a shifting of your threshold of fear. At each step, you begin at a lower level of arousal than was previously possible. By keeping fear at this low level, you can apply relaxation techniques that will become associated with that item in the fear hierarchy. Keeping the fear at a low level is the key to making the relaxation response work. For that reason, it is important not to skip any steps and to go slowly enough so that you have an opportunity to forge a strong link of association between the item in your hierarchy and your ability to relax.

Most people are pleased—and surprised—to discover that they actually learn to relax better, faster, and more completely as they approach the top of their hierarchy. There is a good reason for this. The more you practice the relaxation techniques, the more adept you will become at them. As you approach the top of the hierarchy where the fear is the

---

*Don't be too concerned with how accurately you can judge your SUD rating. The SUD scale is not a precise tool. It is simply a way of helping to clarify your own general impression of your anxiety level.

strongest, you should have begun to truly master relaxation, even in relatively stressful situations that measure above 60 on the SUD scale.

Another factor is also working in your favor as you near the top of your fear hierarchy. You will have discovered that you can cope with fear in ways other than avoidance. This realization acts as positive reinforcement for changing avoidance behavior. As you draw nearer and nearer your fear, the learning procedure actually gets easier and easier.

MOVING CLOSER TO YOUR FEARS

1. Sit in a quiet comfortable room. You will need the stack of index cards on which you have constructed your fear hierarchy. If you use a tape recorder in your relaxation exercises, you should have that too.

2. Start by relaxing. When you can achieve a SUD rating of less than 15, you can proceed. Do not begin the following steps while your SUD level is above 15 to 20.

3. When you feel well relaxed (SUD level of 0 to 15), pick up the first card in your hierarchy. Read it. Close your eyes, and imagine that you are actually in the situation described on the card. Be as graphic as you can in picturing the scene. (Do not picture *watching* yourself in the scene. Rather, imagine actually being there. Imagine the other people who might be there, the furnishings, smells, sounds, and whatever else is appropriate.) The more nearly your image matches the reality, the better this technique will work for you. Picture the scene for no more than five to ten seconds. Then stop.

4. Assess your present SUD level. It is quite possible that your SUD rating will be as low as before you pictured the scene in the hierarchy. If so, close your eyes, and imagine the scene again. Picture it in your mind for thirty seconds. Be

sure to picture only the scene described on the card. Do not get carried away and start moving up through the hierarchy of scenes. If you still have no increase, go on to the next card, and repeat the procedure.

5. If you sense your SUD rating rising by more than 5 points while you are picturing the scene, begin your relaxation procedure while keeping the scene in focus for thirty seconds. When you stop imagining the scene, if your SUD rating is still above 15, repeat the relaxation procedure. Should your SUD rating *increase* more than 10 points after you picture any scene in the hierarchy, you may have to revise the hierarchy by adding an intermediate step; or, you may be trying to go too fast. Slow down, drop back a level, and see if that helps.

6. When you can picture a scene in the hierarchy for up to thirty seconds with no appreciable rise in your SUD rating, you are ready to go on to the next card.

7. During the early sessions, you may be able to do as many as five or six scenes in your hierarchy. That's good, but don't push yourself. Going a little bit slower than you have to won't hurt, but going too fast can wreck all the good you have done.

8. As you get into sessions where you are working higher up in the fear hierarchy, don't try to do more than one scene per session. Be on the lookout for any large increase, and be prepared to modify your program if you hit a stumbling block.

9. Never end a session with an increase in your SUD rating. If your time is up and so is your SUD level, drop back one scene in the hierarchy and end on that one. That way you can always end each session on a positive, successful note.

10. Only when you have mastered every step in the hierarchy—that is, when you can visualize the most fearful

scene with less than a 10-point increase—should you attempt to try any part of the actual situation. When you do begin working in the real situation, continue to take every step gradually. You may feel confident and ready, but *take your time*. The last thing you need is a premature failure that will shake your confidence.

BUILDING A PROGRAM THAT WORKS

You now have the basics for working with fear. All that remains is to put everything into an overall program that will keep you on the right track and reinforce your progress. Let's start by looking at an example that illustrates how a good program works. We will look at the program that Liz M. used to overcome her fear of riding the subways.

The first thing Liz did was to set aside three half-hour periods a week to spend working on her fear problem. Rather than leave the schedule to chance, she marked on her calendar the days she would practice her exercises. Since she was often tired in the evening after a full day at the office, she decided to take time in the morning when she was fresh.

She spent the first week-and-a-half writing her fear hierarchy. Because her fear had several components, she had to carefully analyze which aspects of the situation she could vary in order to decrease her fear to manageable levels. She started by gradually increasing the amount of time she spent in the subway environment. At first, she would only walk up to the entrance and walk away again. Next, she would walk down the stairs. Then, she would stand in the station for longer periods of time. Later, she would ride increasingly greater distances on the subway.

Liz, realizing that one aspect of riding the subway that disturbed her most was the feeling of being hemmed in by so many people, planned to choose times when the crowds would be light and to slowly work her way up to rush-hour crowds. Finally, she decided that she would feel easier if her best friend rode with her at first, so she wrote that into her hierarchy. When she had written her first hierarchy, she saw that the gaps were too large near the top. So she added a few more steps.

Liz selected rewards that got better and better as she progressed. She then prepared a program chart like that shown in Figure 6-2. (Of course, the comments were not filled in until she actually began to carry out the program.) In addition to the program chart, Liz kept a diary of what happened at each session. In that way, she was able to keep constant track of her progress.

During the next two weeks, Liz learned the relaxation techniques. She found that in the privacy of her own room, she had very little trouble getting down to a SUD rating of 0 to 10. She then felt she was ready to begin systematic desensitization.

When Liz began to imagine the scenes in her hierarchy, she discovered that the scenes at the lower end did not cause her SUD level to rise noticeably. Thus, she was able to do the first four steps in one session. However, when she got above the 60-level, she could do no more than one step per session. At the 90-level, she had to spend four sessions before she began to feel comfortable imagining the scene. She spent three more sessions at the final level of 100.

When Liz began to carry out the steps in her hierarchy in real situations, she was amazed at how much calmer she felt. Still, she decided not to take any chances so she worked through each step very gradually. At first, she felt a little strange doing her relaxation exercises on the subway. But then she made an interesting discovery: everyone was so

SUD Rating	Task	Goal No.	Reward	Date Started	Date Completed Comfortably	Comments
100	Riding alone to work	9	Dinner and movie with office friends			
	Riding to work with friend	8	Extra-nice lunch			
90	Riding alone for one stop only	7	Dinner and movie with friend			
	Riding with friend during off-peak hours	6	Movie with friend			
80	Riding one stop with friend during off-peak hours	5	Dinner with friend			
70						
60	Getting on and off before doors close	4	Have friend over for evening			
50						

SUD Rating	Task	Goal No.	Reward	Date Started	Date Completed Comfortably	Comments
40 30	Waiting for subway	3	Spend quiet evening listening to records			
20 10	Walking down stairs	2	Buy favorite magazine			
0	Walking up to subway entrance	1	Buy favorite chocolate candy bar			

Figure 6-2. Liz M.'s systematic desensitization program for overcoming her fear of riding subways.

SUD Rating	Task	Goal No.	Reward	Date Started	Date Completed Comfortably	Comments
100	Riding alone to work	9	Dinner and movie with office friends	November 9	December 1	YIPPEEEEE!!!
	Riding to work with friend	8	Extra-nice lunch	October 8	November 8	Didn't like crowds, but felt in control. Beats staying home.
90	Riding alone for one stop only	7	Dinner and movie with friend	October 5	October 5	Easy. Thought about dinner and movie, and forgot to be scared.
	Riding with friend during off-peak hours	6	Movie with friend	August 15	September 30	Not much different than No. 5. Turned out to be fun. Went to museum.
80	Riding one stop with friend during off-peak hours	5	Dinner with friend	June 15	August 15	Took longer because I could only go on weekends. Not nearly as bad as I thought it would be.
70						
60	Getting on and off before doors close	4	Have friend over for evening	June 12	June 14	Not much different than waiting. Easy.
50						

SUD Rating	Task	Goal No.	Reward	Date Started	Date Completed Comfortably	Comments
40 30	Waiting for subway	3	Spend quiet evening listening to records	June 6	June 11	Knowing that I wasn't really going to get on made it easier. Took several days to get used to noise.
20 10	Walking down stairs	2	Buy favorite magazine	June 2	June 5	Felt panicky at first, but got right over it.
0	Walking up to subway entrance	1	Buy favorite chocolate candy bar	June 1	June 1	Really easy.

Figure 6-3. Liz M.'s comments indicate her progress through her systematic desensitization program.

absorbed in what he or she was doing that she was not even noticed. Her comments as shown in Figure 6-3 are the best indication of the success of her program.

Liz's program illustrates several valuable points. Let's summarize what they are.

1. Set a schedule, and keep to it. If you don't make the time available, you will never have the time. As with any learning process, overcoming a fear is best done on a regular and consistent basis.

2. Keep records of your progress. A chart on the wall is a highly visible reminder that you have a contract with yourself to accomplish a task. Also, the chart will serve as a form of reinforcement because it will make your progress more visible.

3. Be good to yourself by providing rewards all along the way. In learning any complex task, people are more easily discouraged at a lower end of the learning scale. The early steps sometimes seem only loosely related to the end goal. A system of reinforcements associated with the attainment of each goal in your program is a good way to avoid early discouragement.

One useful trick in planning reinforcements is to use your achievement of a goal as a stepping stone to something you particularly enjoy doing—having dinner with friends, going to a concert, buying something that you want. As you attain higher goals in your program, you will discover that there is additional reinforcement when you find yourself able to accomplish things that are important in your life and from your own heightened sense of self-esteem.

4. Tell a friend about your program. This is valuable because you deepen your own committment to the program by telling someone else about it. In addition, you have someone with whom to discuss your progress. Sometimes when we are stuck on a problem, it is because we are too

close to see it objectively. A friend who can view the problem from the outside, without being involved in it, may be able to suggest things that we are overlooking. Also, a friend can be an additional source of encouragement and reinforcement.

PROTECTING YOUR GAINS

Be prepared to deal with setbacks as you pursue your program. The best way to deal with them is to know that they are bound to occur and that they are a normal part of any learning experience. Setbacks occur because human behavior is not 100 percent constant; it varies with countless factors—how rested we are, the state of our health, the weather, and so on.

In the beginning, attempt to attain your goals only under optimum conditions. If you are tired, or if you just had a fight with your boss, it might be better to put off your assault on a higher goal until things are better. Discouragement leads to failure. Encouragement leads to success.

It's a good idea to base your expectations on your performance on your worst day. That way, for the most part, you'll be pleasantly surprised to find that you do better than you anticipated.

A single successful attainment of a goal does not necessarily ensure all future success. Only repeated successes under varying conditions should count as full attainment.

Be prepared to back off occasionally from any goal that is especially difficult to reach. If you try before you feel ready for it, you risk failure and loss of your previous gains. Try to analyze why you are having difficulty attaining the goal. The most common reason is that you have not made the steps gradual enough. In that case, simply revise your program by adding one or more intermediate steps.

Be assertive enough to not let others endanger the success of your program. *Well-meaning friends and relatives may try to push you faster than you are prepared to go. You must be firm in not letting them unduly influence you.* In addition, the program that you develop will place certain constraints on your life while you are working up to your end goal. Only by being firm with yourself and with people who for some reason, would cause you to deviate from the program, can you hope for success.

Assertion is a problem in many fear cases, and so we have devoted Chapter 8 to the subject. You will discover that it is easier than you think to tell people how you expect them to behave toward you.

Keep practicing the techniques presented in this chapter. Each step along the way is important. If you do not keep up with the necessary exercises that you will be learning here, you may find that you cannot progress beyond a certain point short of your desired goal. Only through continued practice and reiteration of these exercises under a variety of conditions can you be assured of success.

CAN YOU REALLY DO IT ALONE?

If you were to seek professional help from a behavior therapist, you would very likely develop a program similar to the one we have described. The therapist would assist you in analyzing your program, refining it, and making sure that the steps from one goal to the next are small enough to be manageable.

For many reasons, you may not wish to seek professional help. You may not think that your fear is that severe. You might prefer to handle the situation on your own and avoid a therapist's fees. Whatever your reasons, you should be aware that professional help is available if you need it. If you find that you require professional help, you will be pleased to know that your attempt to analyze your fears in the manner described here will be useful in getting your professional treatment off to a faster, better start.

A final word of encouragement. Imagination and creativity play a role in fears. The situations that we imagine and the dangers that we create in our own mind are a large part of what makes us fearful. Using the guidelines presented here, together with some imagination and creativity, is all that is needed to build a workable program for controlling your fear.

Additional Information

Behavior Therapy Techniques, Joseph Wolpe, Pergamon Press, 1966.
Self-Directed Systematic Desensitization, W.W. Wenrich, H.H. Dawley, and D.A. General, Behaviordelia, 1976.

7.
THOUGHT-STOPPING —THE CONTROL OF OBSESSIVE FEARS

A person who worries needlessly about unlikely or implausible events is experiencing a type of fear that is called *obsession*. Examples of obsessions are constant concern over coming into contact with germs (in a relatively sanitary environment), or preoccupation with having a heart attack in the absence of any physical evidence, or continual fantasies about death by means of a plane crash or auto accident, or at the hands of muggers.

Just as phobias are typically the exaggerated outgrowth of adaptive fears, obsessions tend to be, at least nominally, related to matters of legitimate concern. Obsessions are irrational, not in their subject matter, but in the degree of importance that we ascribe to them and the disproportionate impact that they have on our lives.

Unlike phobias, obsessions require no specific stimulus or situation to trigger the fear response. Rather, a person seizes upon some imagined threat and becomes obsessed with fearful thoughts to the exclusion of all reasonable counterarguments—often to the point of being unable to work, relax, or enjoy otherwise pleasant pursuits. In such instances, the problem is not so much *what* the person fears but rather the *thought* of fear.

When we obsess, we insult our nervous system. The insult comes from placing ourselves in a position of great stress, while doing absolutely nothing useful to alter the stress-producing situation. Not only are we doing nothing useful in obsessing, we may be increasing the likelihood of creating the very situation we fear. A person can become so obsessed with fear of losing control that the eventual outcome will be a loss of control.

Planning our lives so as to avoid mishaps in the future is useful behavior. Obsessing about things that either have little chance of happening or are out of our control is useless and often harmful.

THOUGHTS OF FEAR

Frank P. is a 46-year-old accountant. He is married and has a 14-year-old son. Early one morning, Frank was awakened by the telephone. The caller was the wife of his closest friend Jim, and she was sobbing hysterically. Her husband, who was the same age as Frank and apparently in good health, had suffered a heart attack during the night and died on the way to the hospital. Frank was stunned, as he had just seen Jim the previous day, and he had appeared to be fine.

Frank himself had always enjoyed excellent health. He had no history of heart trouble. He exercised regularly, was not overweight, and did not smoke. A few months after his friend's death, however, he began to complain of chest pains. He went to his family doctor for a physical checkup and was pronounced exceptionally fit. Not satisfied with that opinion, however, Frank consulted a specialist and again was assured that he had nothing to worry about.

Sometimes, while sitting in his office, Frank would put his hand to his chest to feel his heart beating. He thought it might be beating too fast. Each time Frank thought of his heart, he pictured Jim, remembering how healthy he had seemed on the day before his death.

Frank began to worry about his wife and son. He took out a large insurance policy, even though it strained the family budget. He no longer played softball with his son, and gave up his weekend tennis. In addition, he stopped exercising and no longer made love to his wife for fear of taxing his heart. He even traded in his manual lawn mower for a power mower, and then traded that in for a riding mower.

Frank began to sleep poorly. As his tension grew, some of the very symptoms that he was concerned about were created. For instance, his lack of exercise caused his weight to go up. In addition, his blood pressure increased. Thus, he has become so obsessed with fear of a heart attack, that he may be well on his way to creating the very problem that he seeks to avoid.

THOUGHTS AND ATTENTION

When friends and family caution Frank not to worry so much, he takes refuge behind a common excuse, ''I can't help what I think.'' We all tend to believe that our bodily actions are pretty much under our control, whereas our thoughts are much less so. A moment of reflection about our thinking processes shows how mistaken this belief is. We can and do exercise power of selection over our thoughts.

A busy executive trying to solve a business problem may have her entire attention focused on that problem. If a colleague interrupts her, she may choose from among several courses of action: she may (1) stop what she is doing and have a conversation; (2) mumble some response indicating that her attention is somewhere else; or (3) explain that she is busy right now and go back to thinking about the problem. She is exercising selectivity over her thoughts. She *can* help what she thinks.

Similarly, a student may be thinking hard about an algebra problem while keeping an eye on the clock. At exactly 4:30 p.m., the student shifts his attention from algebra and begins to plan the evening: what to have for dinner, where to go afterward, what to wear, and so on.

These two examples show how we direct our attention from one set of thoughts to another. Using these as our model, let's consider what Frank might do to shift his attention away from his imagined heart trouble.

STOPPING THOUGHTS OF FEAR

To cope with obsessive thoughts of fear, we use a deceptively simple technique called *thought-stopping*. The technique consists basically of three parts: (1) to become aware of when an obsessive thought intrudes upon our lives; (2) to then learn to consciously direct our attention to some other aspect of the environment; and (3) to develop a systematic program that will strengthen and enhance this response until we are in full control of obsessive thoughts.

To start, allot a period of time for a first session with yourself. Choose a time when you are not likely to be disturbed. If you wish, take the telephone off the hook. Find a quiet, comfortable place to sit.

Have available some sort of prop that is capable of holding your attention, such as television, a book, or any other activity that can command your attention. As soon as you become aware of the obsessive thought, say out loud, "Stop," and try to direct your attention away from the thought and toward the prop you have chosen. Note that you can, indeed, divert your attention from the obsessive thought, even if it is only for the few seconds required to think about saying "Stop," actually saying it, and trying to redirect your attention. *A few seconds may not seem like much at first, but it is a beginning. As you practice the technique, you will discover that the intervals between obsessive thoughts become longer and that the frequency of the thoughts, in any given period, diminishes.*

Having noted that you can redirect your attention by saying "Stop" aloud, try saying it to yourself. In fact, you may want to develop some sort of stop image, for example, bright red letters or a large red stop sign with flashing lights. The more vivid the image you choose, the more diverting it is likely to be, and the better the technique will work for you.

You may discover at first that the obsessive thoughts tumble over you almost more rapidly than you can extinguish them with your thought-stopping techniques. This treadmill effect is to be expected. By the very act of sitting down to cope with your problems of obsession, you are, in effect, calling attention to the obsession, reminding yourself of it. Don't be discouraged. Although many people find that their first session of thought-stopping yields substantial results, many more find it takes several sessions—and sometimes as long as several weeks—before they begin to note real progress.

Like all of the techniques presented in this book, the best results will be achieved if you practice them systematically. It is important to keep records, which serve as a visible reminder to keep up with the practice as well as strong reinforcement as you note your own progress.

BUILDING A THOUGHT-STOPPING PROGRAM

To pursue a thought-stopping program, you should buy a small counter like those used to count knitting stitches.

These inexpensive devices can be purchased in most five-and-tens.

Carry the counter with you. Each time you become aware of obsessive thoughts, say to yourself, "Stop," and press the counter. At the end of the day, make a note of the number of times you pressed the counter. Within a couple of weeks, you should notice that the number of times that you have obsessive thoughts is gradually diminishing. There is nothing magical about this. It is simply a basic law of behavior that punishment (saying stop) tends to extinguish a behavior and reward (seeing your progress and experiencing the pleasure associated with reaching the milestones of your program) tends to enhance and encourage a behavior.

The use of a counter will have several beneficial effects on your developing thought-stopping powers. In the first place, the simple act of recording the number of times you say "Stop" on the counter introduces a new element of behavior. Any time a new form of behavior is introduced, it serves to focus attention on itself and, therefore, away from the obsessive thoughts. In addition, the counter will provide the data for your records, and the records will, in turn, be a source of reinforcement and reward.

You may find it helpful to establish additional rewards in your program as motivators. For example, after observing thought-stopping behavior for a couple of days and noting the number of times that you record on the counter, you might set a goal. If you reduce your obsessive thoughts from 80 to 60 a day, for example, you might reward yourself with a dinner out or an evening with a friend. A drop to 40 might warrant going to a concert you want to hear. Keep rewarding yourself until you feel that your level of obsession is low enough that you are in control of your thoughts.

Some people are inclined to worry about what others around them will think if they see them using the counter.

In the first place, be reassured that most people won't notice. The counters, which are small and unobtrusive, make very little noise. Second, of the few people that do notice, most will not ask what you are doing and, the few that do ask can almost always be put off with a casual remark such as, "I'm just using this to help me keep track of some things."

OBSESSION AS A PART OF OTHER FEARS

Obsessions can also play a role in phobic behavior by fueling the fires of phobic thought. Let's consider obsession as a component of the phobic process.

Jenny W. is preparing to leave on vacation. She's flying to the West Coast where she will spend two weeks visiting friends, seeing some of the tourist attractions, and soaking up the sun on a warm, southern California beach. Although she is looking forward to her vacation, she is not looking forward to traveling. Jenny is afraid of flying.

Upon leaving the house to go to the airport, Jenny sighs to herself, "Oh...my life is so good and safe, why am I messing things up by risking my life on this trip?" This type of thinking persists and becomes more frequent as she drives to the airport. "There hasn't been a plane crash in almost a year—I bet we're due for one, and I'll be on it....I really don't need to take this trip—why the hell am I doing this to myself?" She has visions of herself becoming so frightened on the airplane that she begins to cry and scream uncontrollably, embarrassing herself and the other passengers. In the waiting room of the airport and while boarding the plane, she fantasizes about the plane's exploding in midair. She sees herself being engulfed by flames and feels a sinking feeling in the pit of her stomach. She forces herself to get on the plane and straps herself into her seat. Her face is ashen, her hands are shaking, and she is on the verge of losing control.

For all her worrying and obsessing, Jenny has done nothing to alter the probability of what will happen to the airplane. What she has accomplished is to create a situation in which the very thing she is terrified of—namely, losing control out of fear—is more likely to occur.

Obsessions feed on themselves. The more we allow ourselves to dwell on unpleasant, worrisome thoughts, the greater our obsession with them becomes. To use a common analogy, if you scratch an itch, it may make it feel better at first; however, if you continue to scratch, it will become irritated, and the itch will become worse. If we leave an itch alone, or direct our attention away from it, very often it will go away on its own. The same thought-stopping techniques used when the obsession is the fear can also be applied to obsessions as they affect phobias.

Tell yourself "Stop." Consciously direct your attention to other things, and keep practicing. A useful hint is to keep from obsessing by focusing on your end goal. For example, if Jenny had focused on how much fun she was going to have in California, she would have found her attention related to that rather than to the obsessive thoughts that she experienced.

Similarly with other phobias, direct your attention to the end result that you are striving to achieve. Think about how you will increase your self-esteem and confidence upon achieving that goal. Think about the new freedom that you will introduce into your life by gaining greater control over your thoughts. You will be pleasantly surprised to find that you have less time for obsessing.

MENTAL BARGAINING

We mention one final instance in which thought-stopping is appropriate, namely, striking a mental bargain with yourself. Sitting on the airplane, Jenny holds the following conversation in her mind, "God, if this plane just lands safely, then I'm really going to work on improving my relationship with my family when I get home." Having struck this bargain with herself (and perhaps some omnipotent second party), she finds, miraculously, that her fear is reduced. However, on the return trip, Jenny is even more afraid of the plane than before, and the bargain she strikes with herself is more elaborate.

Mental bargaining is effective in momentarily reducing fear for several reasons. First, a mental bargain creates the *illusion* that you are in control of a situation in which lack of control is often a cause of the fear. By striking the bargain, you are at least doing *something*. Second, the mere process of bargaining is distracting and interrupts the obsession, thus reducing the discomfort. Third, perhaps most important, the belief in the bargain reduces the fear momentarily. The difficulty comes from the fact that the fear reduction simply reinforces the bargaining procedure and the tendency to obsess. Another mental bargain is called for, and still another. Each step of the way, you escalate to higher levels of fear because of the reinforcement that occurs. Mental bargaining (see Figure 7-1) is no substitute for thought-stopping.

Figure 7-1. The closed loop of mental bargaining.

8.
STANDING UP FOR YOURSELF

People with fear problems sometimes experience a related group of difficulties, which psychologists refer to as *assertive problems*. A lack of assertiveness may have its roots in social fear (that is, fears of interacting with other people), or it may be a side effect of some other fear. Fearful people may be unassertive because of what they fear or because they are ashamed to show their fear. An inability to assert yourself in appropriate situations allows, and even invites, others to take advantage of you, to play upon and increase your fear.

Like other types of fears, unassertiveness can needlessly limit and degrade your life. Unassertive children are frequently the targets of bullies. Adults with assertion problems are usually subjected to somewhat more subtle forms of bullying by insecure bosses, aggressive salespeople, domineering family and friends, and thoughtless strangers.

To be assertive does not mean to be aggressive, argumentative, or overbearing. It simply means to stand up for your rights and to feel comfortable about it. If you are adequately asssertive, you have no trouble telling others how you expect them to behave toward you. An inability to do this can have a variety of unpleasant effects ranging from lowered self-esteem, to a lack of goal achievement, and even to the acceptance of physical abuse.

If you are using the techniques described in earlier chapters to develop a program for overcoming fears, you may need to develop assertive techniques that will allow you to stick with the program. Well-meaning friends and relatives may try to push you too fast on your program—and *you* have to be able to tell them to stop. A carefully planned program can be ruined if you allow yourself to skip steps. So, stand up for yourself and for your right to overcome your fear at your own pace. Anything else may lead to failure.

WHY ASSERTION WORKS

Two theories seek to explain why assertive behavior is useful in overcoming fears. One contends that assertion acts as an ''inhibitory response'' to fear, that it effectively blocks feelings of fear in much the same way as relaxation does. According to this theory, assertion and anxiety are physiologically incompatible: a person cannot be fearful and assertive at the same time.

Another quite different theory holds that assertion simply creates an improved social situation that is less conducive to the maintenance of fears and anxieties. To exaggerate only slightly, the theory suggests—rather plausibly—that having a friendly conversation is superior to cowering in a corner as a means of coping with fear. Whatever the theoretical basis may be for using assertive techniques to deal with fears, the clinical evidence is indisputable—it gets results in many instances.

Numerous books and articles, both popular and academic,

have been written on assertive behavior. Some of these writings are quite entertaining as well as informative. Stephen Potter's books on the art of one-upmanship offer a perceptive analysis of nonassertive behavior and a gold mine of hilarious solutions. Even the more staid textbooks can make for some interesting reading on how to deal with the problem, as with the following case history.

Mr. G.F., aged 21 years, was a clerk in a firm of lawyers where he was receiving exceptionally good training and experience. The senior partner, however, appeared to take sadistic delight in finding fault with his work and would deliver unnecessarily lengthy lectures on petty details. The patient, an asthmatic, found that on nights following these "excruciating monologues," he invariably suffered from severe bronchial tension. Therapeutic attention was then devoted to the implementation of subtle tactics which might serve to discourage the employer's prolonged and denigrating lectures. Mr. G.F. was instructed to make casual inquiries from the secretaries and other office personnel regarding the senior partner's idiosyncrasies and possible vulnerabilities. At the next session, the patient informed the therapist that the senior partner was reputed to be a hypochondriac. The therapist asked Mr. G.F. whether he was able to feign a worried expression when his principal next engaged in one of his triades and to interject with some assumed statement of concern with regard to the state of his employer's health. Three weeks later, Mr. G.F. was jubilant. He described an occasion when his employer lit his pipe and settled back in his customary manner to deliver one of his harangues. Mr. G.F. recounted how he had riveted his gaze on his employer's left cheek and (approximately 10 minutes later) his employer had demanded to know what he was staring at. "I put on a worried frown as though my discovery was too dreadful to repeat and said, 'Nothing sir. Excuse me for asking, sir, but are you feeling quite well?' The senior partner was reported to have replied, 'Why, what's wrong?', whereupon Mr. G.F. said, 'Nothing, sir. Nothing at all.' The interview was terminated less than two minutes later. Mr. G.F. completed the remaining 18 months of his apprenticeship without further incident and was offered a junior partnership upon qualifying.*

The literature on assertion is filled with similar ploys and counterploys for gaining an upper hand over people. We have no intention of trying to distill this rich literature in this book. We can only touch upon the subject as it relates specifically to coping with fear problems. We concentrate on two areas: (1) assertiveness as a means of increasing your control in certain social situations that are fear-provoking, and (2) assertion as a way of keeping others from interfering with your ability to carry out a program for overcoming your fears. Without attempting to be complete, we can focus on some of the social and verbal skills that you can acquire to alter the way people treat you in your efforts to cope with fears.

UP THE ORGANIZATION THROUGH ASSERTION

Many people feel frightened and intimidated in totally impersonal situations over which they seem to have no control. We are all familiar with the animosity that is commonly expressed toward computers, bureaucratic organizations, and large companies in which everything is "run by the book." Frequently, assertive behavior in certain of

---

*From Wolpe, *Behavior Therapy Techniques,* Pergamon Press, 1966.

these situations can create a point of human contact that breaks down the impersonal and threatening facade. The discovery that we are dealing with people and not preprogrammed robots can sometimes lead to a lessening of hostility, a decrease in anxiety, and a feeling of greater control over our own lives.

When Sarah first began to feel pangs of anxiety in the supermarket, she was almost unaware of it. The symptoms were very subtle. She found herself short-tempered with her young daughter, and she was unable to concentrate on what she was doing. She felt tense, nervous, and insecure. As her anxiety grew, she began to shop more often at the convenience store near her house, even though the prices were a little higher. With increased frequency, she would ask her husband to ''pick up a few things on the way home.'' She also prevailed upon friends who were going shopping to pick up a few things as a favor to her. The more adept she became at avoiding supermarkets, the more her fear of going into one increased.

One Friday, when her in-laws were coming for dinner, Sarah's husband called to say that he had to work late and could not stop at the supermarket to buy the items she had requested that morning. She would have to do the shopping herself. She checked with a couple of friends, but they were not going shopping and thus couldn't help her. The corner store didn't have what she needed. However, rather than face a supermarket, Sarah changed the menu. While having to switch from beef stroganoff to meat loaf is hardly a crippling result of fear, Sarah recognized the irrationality of her fear and the strong hold that it had gained over her. She decided to seek professional help.

The first meeting with the therapist disclosed that Sarah's anxieties were related to a number of small fears: she worried that she would spend more than her budgeted grocery allowance, and she was afraid of buying bad fruits and vegetables or, equally dangerous, of incurring the anger of the store manager by picking up produce to inspect it. She became nervous waiting in the checkout line, afraid that she might be late for whatever she had to do next, or afraid that she would not have enough money when the price of the groceries was totaled. In general, she felt the supermarket was an ideal arena for disaster and that she had no control over the multitude of bad experiences that lurked in wait for her there.

Some initial attempts at relaxation and systematic desensitization were unsuccessful. Since her anxiety levels were generally low enough that she could still enter a supermarket, although with some discomfort, the therapist decided to try assertive training. Sarah was given the task of going into the supermarket, picking up a single item, and asking one of the store personnel if the price were correct as marked. Whatever the answer, she was to say that it seemed too high, put the item back on the shelf, and leave the store. The therapist rehearsed the scene with her, playing the part of a supermarket manager and coaching Sarah in what to say, in using a firm tone of voice, and in looking the manager in the eye.

She was nervous and very tense on her first trial, and actually felt more than a little silly. However, the result was both pleasant and surprising. As she had practiced, she picked up an item—a can of coffee. When she told the manager that the price was too high, he smiled and said, "You're telling me, lady. We've had to switch to drinking tea in my family." He then took her to another aisle and showed her a special that the store was running on another brand of coffee at a slightly lower price. At first flustered, since she had not intended to buy anything, she regained her composure enough to say that the price was still too high. The manager pleasantly agreed that the price of coffee had skyrocketed and that it was probably a good idea for people to cut back on drinking it until the price came down.

Afterward, Sarah's anxieties diminished very rapidly. That simple bit of human contact had cast the supermarket in a whole new light. No longer was it a huge impersonal monster bent on grabbing her money and embarrassing her. As a precaution, however, the therapist recommended a couple of additional trials. So, on another visit to the same store, Sarah asked the manager how to pick out good fruits and vegetables. He quickly showed her how to test lettuce for firmness, to smell cantaloupe to judge ripeness, and to turn tomatoes around to check for bruised spots. Recognizing that Sarah had been fortunate to encounter a helpful manager, the therapist spent a session role-playing what to do in the event of an unpleasant encounter. While her concern about managing the family budget still made Sarah anxious from time to time, the anxiety was in large part offset by her newfound ability to seek out the best buys in the supermarket.

INSPIRING CONFIDENCE THROUGH ASSERTION

Ironically, the very people who most fear making a bad impression on others tend to create the worst impressions. Their lack of confidence shows up in what they say and the way they say it. As a result, they cannot gain the confidence that they seek from others. If you are asking the boss for a raise, you want to inspire confidence that you deserve it. Inviting a new acquaintance to spend an evening with you, you want to exude a sense that it will be enjoyable. When asking a friend for a favor, you have less chance of getting it if your fear of being turned down is so great that your friend misinterprets your motives. As the following example indicates, simple techniques of assertive behavior can be used to impart a heightened sense of confidence and increase your chances for success in social interactions.

Len had worked at the same engineering firm ever since graduating from college 12 years earlier. When the management of the company changed hands, he suddenly found that he was no longer getting interesting projects to work on, his pay increases were smaller, and he was passed over for promotion to division director. He wanted to change jobs but, at the time, firms in the area were firing more engineers than they were hiring. He was lucky to have a job, so he stayed on with the company.

After a few months, the employment situation improved, but Len had severe doubts about his ability to get another job. After all, he reasoned, he wasn't getting any younger and his field of specialization was rather narrow. Nevertheless, he eventually got up the courage to send resumes to a few companies, and, to his surprise, he received two requests for interviews. His anxiety began to build as soon as the date for the first interview was set. By the time the day arrived, Len was virtually in a state of panic. He feared that someone in his old company would find out and that he might be fired—and then he wouldn't get the new job. He worried that perhaps he had not adequately explained his specialty in the resume, and that he would look foolish applying for a job for which he was not qualified. The interview did not go well, and he did not get a job offer. The next one was even worse, so that Len could not bring himself to face another. He became increasingly depressed and eventually sought therapy.

The therapist quickly determined that Len's depression and fears generally revolved around his dissatisfaction with his job and his feelings of helplessness to change the situation. Playing the role of a prospective employer, the therapist had Len act out an interview situation. Len went outside the office, knocked on the door, and was told to come in. He sat down, and the therapist asked the kinds of questions that come up in job interviews. Len's performance was not impressive. His knock was soft and tentative, and he came shambling in, looking at the floor. As the therapist made up questions to ask about Len's previous employment, Len fidgeted with his hands, nervously cracking his knuckles. He mumbled, started sentences without finishing them, and made frequent disparaging remarks about himself, which he tried to treat as jokes by laughing a bit too harshly. Asked to describe his work, Len focused mainly on things that he could not do.

Len and the therapist then reversed roles. With considerable flair and obvious relish, Len played the role of the vice president of personnel; the psychologist became the interviewee, imitating the mannerisms that he had noted in Len. To Len's own surprise, he found himself in complete agreement that he would not give a job to an applicant who made such a poor presentation.

The role-playing made it easier to convince Len that people were reacting less to his qualifications as an engineer than to his manner of presenting himself. Interviewers could not get beyond a bad first impression. The negative image he presented of himself encouraged the negative responses that he feared.

Over the next several sessions, the therapist concentrated on helping Len develop a more positive image of himself. In addition, they continued the role-playing, with the therapist acting as stage director, prompting Len to walk with his head up, to speak in a firmer tone, to make eye contact, and to shake hands with some authority. Some relaxation techniques were also practiced as a means of keeping Len's anxieties down for his next interview. To Len's great surprise, learning to *act* with more confidence actually made him feel more self-assured. Less than two months after starting therapy, Len had another interview. He received a job offer, but it was not at the salary he was hoping for. However, he had developed enough confidence to reject the offer. He talked to several prospective employers and even confronted his boss to find out firsthand what his chances for advancement were. Several months later, Len announced to the therapist that he had decided to accept an offer from another company and that assertive training had paid off in other areas as well, leading to improvements in his social life and his working relations with others.

That Len should have felt a little nervous and frightened going into an interview is not surprising. However, his intense focus on his own fears got in the way of the interview. The assertiveness training really did nothing more than remove some initial barriers that were making it impossible for Len to create a favorable first impression. Given the positive responses that his newly assertive behavior elicited, he rapidly gained confidence. Because he was more relaxed, he was able to think more quickly and respond more appropriately, not only in an interview, but in other social situations as well.

GAINING COOPERATION (AND CONTROL) THROUGH ASSERTION

Anne had lived in a small town in New Hampshire for most of her life. She had never flown in an airplane and had no desire to do so. But when her daughter's husband was transferred to California, air travel became a necessity if Anne wanted to see her daughter and young grandson. Her first flight to the West Coast was spent in tight-lipped silence, gripping the armrest. She did not move from her seat the entire flight and did not eat anything because the meal was not kosher.

Although she had looked forward to seeing her family, Anne did not enjoy the visit. She refused to go into the city to go shopping with her daughter. She felt uncomfortable about meeting her daughter's new friends. And she spent much of her time fretting about the return trip home. Her daughter sensed that something was wrong and became concerned that her mother might be deterred from future visits if the problems were not resolved. At her daughter's urging, Anne agreed to consult a therapist.

In the initial interview, the therapist quickly realized that Anne's problem was not flight phobia, for she was not afraid of the plane crashing. In fact, she regarded air travel as relatively safe. Neither did she appear to suffer from claustrophobia (which might have been an element in her anxiety over planes and large city crowds). After some discussion, it became apparent that Anne was acutely uncomfortable in situations where she had to rely on strangers to do things for her. In an airplane, a large city, or a department store, she felt anxious that she might need to go to the bathroom and not know where it was, or that she might need a drink of water, or that people would be annoyed with her if she asked them for directions or assistance. She admitted that she had been terrified that her daughter might not be at the airport when she arrived and that she did not go into the city with her for fear that they might become separated accidentally.

The therapist started by acquainting Anne with several types of assertive behavior that would help her to feel comfortable traveling, visiting large cities, or being in crowds. Much of the therapy focused on rehearsing the types of interactions that she might expect to encounter.

When the time came for the trip home, Anne concentrated hard on the therapist's advice. When she boarded the plane, she told the flight attendant that she was afraid to fly. Anne was pleasantly surprised when the attendant changed her assigned seat, explaining, "You'll find the ride a little smoother near the front, and I'll be able to keep an eye on you there. If you feel yourself getting anxious, just tell me."

In addition, just as the therapist had suggested, Anne

asked the flight attendant for a kosher meal. She was told that the airline provided for just such a contingency.

Although the flight was crowded and the flight attendant was busy, she made a point of stopping to chat with Anne several times, to ask how she was feeling, and to reassure her that everything was all right. Anne discovered that, with very little anxiety, she was able to get up to go to the bathroom, get a magazine, or simply stretch her legs. As her anxiety became less pronounced, Anne was able to strike up a conversation with her seat mate. The time passed more quickly than on the flight out—and much more pleasantly.

Anne no longer felt as if she were a piece of freight being transported from one place to another. Through her interaction with the flight attendant, Anne realized that the airline people were eager to please her and to make her feel comfortable. This realization went a long way toward reducing her anxieties.

Admitting a fear to a stranger requires an act of assertiveness. You are saying, in effect, ''I hope you will behave differently toward me to keep me from experiencing undue discomfort.'' When faced with such a request, most people will make an effort to treat you differently. But people are not mind readers. They need to be told what you expect of them—and this requires assertion. Also, by speaking up and asking for the things you need and want, you gain a feeling of control. You become the master of the situation, rather than having the situation control you. By a simple act of assertiveness, Anne set in motion a sequence of events that freed her from what would have been a severe limitation on her life. By learning to speak up for herself, she was far better able to make the long trip back and forth to California in comfort and in control.

VERBAL SKILLS AS ASSERTIVE BEHAVIOR

As with other aspects of learning assertive behavior, the verbal skills alone are the subject of entire books. Let us consider some of the most common ones that may be useful in overcoming fears.

Speak up. Practice speaking clearly, forcefully. Don't mumble or slur words. There are several reasons for this. It makes a better impression on people, and it lets them hear and understand you. People can't change their behavior toward you if they don't hear what you say, if they don't understand your words, or if you fail to get their attention by speaking too softly.

Ask questions. Don't be afraid to ask questions. If you don't know the answer, there is a very good chance that the question needs to be asked. In fact, very often you will find that a great many other people ask the same questions. You will generally find that people are happy to answer most questions. Of course, be prepared to run into an occasional grouch who will seem unbearably put out by having to answer a question—but just remember that you have a right to know the answer.

Examples of questions that people hesitate to raise are: how much does it cost? where is the bathroom? why does it take so long to get the item I ordered? what does a guarantee on this item *really* mean? Unfortunately, some people tend to feel that, if they don't understand something, it is their own fault because they are stupid. More often than not, the fault lies elsewhere. For instance, there may be inadequate signs to direct you to where you want to go, or the service that you have a right to expect may be genuinely lousy, or a purported piece of information, such as a warranty may be written in such jargon that it is incomprehensible. In asking questions, you'll find that you get the best results if you speak up. Busy people usually don't mind answering sensible questions, but they may be annoyed if they have to work to understand what is being asked of them.

Finally, don't be afraid to ask questions out of fear of seeming dumb. The only stupid people in the world are those who don't ask questions because they already know all the answers.

Let people know how you feel. People are not mind readers. If you want someone to know that he or she is doing something to make you unhappy, say so. A man smoking a cigar in a crowded elevator may not be striving to be offensive. He may simply not be aware that he is offending someone. Often, people who discover that they are inadvertently disturbing someone else are genuinely sorry and are anxious to change their behavior to make it more acceptable. Of course, there are exceptions. The rock music addict may not take kindly to being asked to keep his music to himself. A husband and wife in the heat of a loud argument may be less than thrilled to learn that they are disturbing your sleep. Letting others know that their actions are displeasing to you will not cure all annoying behavior. But it is a good place to start.

One of the most successful of all assertive techniques is the use of praise to reward people for behaving in ways that you want them to. Letting someone know that he or she has done something to make you happy is just as important as complaining of actions that displease you. Remember that one of the three main ways in which learning occurs is through reward. Each time you make someone feel good by praising behavior that you find agreeable, you reinforce that behavior and increase the likelihood of its recurrence.

Rehearsing. If there are specific situations in which you have assertive problems, try rehearsing the scene before you go into it. Simply worrying about a situation before you go into it does nothing to prepare you for it. In fact, it probably makes matters worse because you don't go in relaxed. Write out what you want to say, and learn it so that you can say it without notes. Think about the questions that might be raised, and be prepared to answer at least the most obvious ones. There's nothing to bolster confidence like being prepared.

NONVERBAL ASSERTIVE TECHNIQUES

In the same way that many animals have clearly defined pecking orders, humans also have unwritten social rules that establish their stature in relation to others. The literature is filled with descriptions of dominant and submissive behaviors by which you raise or lower yourself relative to another person. We will touch upon a few of the most common ones, to make you aware of what they are and to stimulate you to think how they might be used to your advantage.

Your facial expressions, your body movements, what you do with your hands—all say something about your feelings. If they say you are anxious, fearful, or nervous, the effect you produce on other people will be negative. They will tend to be suspicious, uncooperative, and aloof. By contrast, if your body language radiates calm confidence, you are more apt to get the response you desire. As an added bonus, when you act calm and confident, there is a strong tendency for your emotions to fall into step so that you also *feel* more calm and confident.

Eye contact. Nothing breeds confidence in our society like looking another person in the eye. This simple act of assertiveness is among the most important of all social maneuvers. In fact, eye contact is used by most mammals as a means of asserting dominance. An animal or person who looks a challenger in the eye is proclaiming that he is not afraid. One speculation suggests that only a friend can look you in the eye, and that an enemy watches your hands. If you feel uncomfortable looking directly into another person's eyes, look at the forehead instead.

Appearing calm. When you appear nervous and uncomfortable, you make others feel the same way. For the most part, the best thing to do with hands is nothing. Put them in your lap, and keep them there. That way, they don't wind up covering your mouth, scratching your ear, or adjusting your clothes. If you use your hands to gesture, it's probably a good idea to rehearse in front of a mirror. And if you keep them still except to make a point, they will have more impact. Also, they will be less likely to go flying off on their own and knock over nearby breakables.

The "home court" advantage. People often find themselves in a state of high anxiety when faced with the necessity of meeting with someone whom they fear will take advantage of them. One of the best ways to deal with this type of fear is to seize the initiative in arranging the meeting. In that way, you can gain the "home court" advantage: you can control not only the time, place, and duration of the meeting, but the tone as well.

In a business situation, for example, a meeting held in

your own office gives you the advantage of sitting behind your desk, clearly a dominant role. You can make the meeting more intimate by seating the other person near the desk, or you can make it more formal by seating the person at some distance from you. Refreshments can be used to add an air of congeniality, or withheld to emphasize a no-nonsense approach. You can control the opening sequences by jumping right in with a difficult question, or by engaging in friendly small talk and working up to the topic more gradually. Whatever approach, the point is that you enhance your ability to control the situation by creating the setting in which you are most likely to succeed in asserting yourself.

BUILDING YOUR OWN ASSERTION PROGRAM

Once again, we caution that we have not tried to be complete in our discussion of assertion, we have only touched upon some of the high spots. If you believe that your fears are related in some way to an assertive problem, you can take several initial steps on your own.

Read. Begin by reading at least two of the popular books on the subject. Any of the books listed at the end of this chapter give a reasonable introduction to start you thinking more systematically about ways of developing assertive behavior.

Analyze. You can sometimes act as your own therapist simply by taking the time to think through a problem in an organized way. This effective approach is so simple and obvious that it gets overlooked.

A good start is to use the relaxation techniques we have described. By sitting in a quiet room and becoming relaxed, you improve your ability to concentrate. Once relaxed, write down descriptions of specific situations in which you feel assertiveness is a problem. Try to group the situations in terms of common factors. In the right kind of peaceful setting, with your body relaxed and your mind focused, a straightforward definition of the problem may be all that is needed to suggest a solution.

In general, you are looking for a solution that will change certain ways in which others behave toward you. And to do this, you probably have to change some aspect of your behavior first. Don't overlook the obvious: a straightforward approach can be very effective. If Mrs. X is making you uncomfortable, try to tell her how you feel and to ask her to behave differently toward you. This solution is by no means infallible, but you may be surprised to learn how often people will cooperate if you tell them in a reasonable way how you want to be treated.

Modeling your behavior. As we mentioned earlier, imitating the behavior of others is a highly effective learning technique. It can be especially advantageous to you in overcoming assertive problems.

Choose as your model someone who is successful in those situations where you have assertive difficulties. Watch how your model handles the situation, and try to do the same on your own. Notice how your model talks—not only what he or she says, but the way it is said. Observe what your model does with hands, feet, and facial expressions. If you feel uncomfortable modeling your behavior after someone else, it may help to remember that you are simply doing at a conscious level the same thing you have been doing at an unconscious level all your life. You are learning by imitation. The only difference is that you are making it work *for* you, not *against* you.

PRACTICE

Assertive behavior needs to be developed as a response—that is, you must be able to summon it upon command. To do this requires practice.

When you have hit upon an assertive technique that feels comfortable to you, use it often. Remember that assertion is not rudeness or bullying. It can be done with politeness, even gentleness. If you don't feel comfortable trying out a technique in public, you can always try it on a friend. If the friend also happens to be your model for assertion, you may pick up some additional valuable pointers.

A good way to practice assertive techniques is with waiters, bus drivers, salespeople, bank tellers, and the countless other people who provide services. The following are good examples of *perfectly acceptable ways* in which you can practice assertion.

Asking a waiter to take back a dish that has not been properly prepared. Be ready to explain why—that it is burned, or raw, or cold.

Asking a bus driver for directions. If you don't understand them, ask more questions.

Telling a bank clerk that an error has been made in your account.

Telling a salesperson that you are returning a defective item.

Telling an auto mechanic that your bill is higher than the estimate.

This brief list should be enough to suggest many more possibilities to you.

As you successfully employ assertive techniques, you

will find that another learning process we discussed earlier is at work: *association*. You will be building a repertoire of successful and adaptive behaviors that in time can be generalized to other aspects of your life. As your confidence grows in your assertive abilities, so will your self-esteem and self-image. And at that point, you have another learning process working in your favor: Learning by rewards. A small change in your behavior can thus create changes in the ways people respond to you and at the same time set in motion the powerful learning forces that can be turned to your advantage.

Additional Information

When I Say No, I Feel Guilty, Manuel J. Smith, Dial Press, 1975.
Don't Say Yes When You Want to Say No, Herbert Fensterheim and Jean Baer, McKay, 1975.

9.
COMPULSIVE BEHAVIOR AND SUPERSTITION

The eccentric millionaire Howard Hughes was reported to be deathly afraid of germs. According to various accounts of his life, he would periodically become so obsessed with fear of contamination, that he would order all of his old clothes to be removed from his home and burned. He would refuse to shake hands for fear of contracting germs, and, numerous times each day, he would interrupt what he was doing to wash his hands, scrubbing them vigorously for long periods. The stories of his later life as a total recluse suggest that his time and efforts were largely devoted to obsessions with germs and to bizzare forms of compulsive behavior that were intended to reduce his anxieties.

Like phobias and obsessions, obsessive-compulsive problems are related to fear. Recall that the phobic avoids a situation or object out of fear, and the obsessive-compulsive ruminates over and over again, thus inducing fear. The obsessive-compulsive adopts a form of behavior, supposedly to deal with the fear, and then becomes afraid *not* to carry out that behavior each time the obsession arises.

Obsessive-compulsive behavior is essentially an anxiety-motivated ritual. Although the obsessive maintains that his problem is his fear (which drives him to perform the ritual), his real problem is the ritual itself. He learns to perform the ritual not only in response to a specific fear, but to any anxiety whatsoever. Hence, the focus of therapy is to stop the ritual or compulsion. For that reason, desensitization techniques are inappropriate, as are the thought-stopping techniques discussed in Chapter 7. Obsessive-compulsive individuals do more than simply incapacitate themselves with worry. They invent new forms of behavior that they believe (incorrectly) will protect them from what they fear, and then use them as general anxiety-reducing strategies.

At first, compulsive behaviors may exhibit some tenuous connection with reality. But over time, the link often becomes vague. For example, according to one account of Howard Hughes's life, the first time that he burned his clothes was when he learned that his wife had contracted a venereal disease. Although VD is not transmitted by clothing, Hughes could well have believed that he was acting with reasonable precaution. However, in later life he continued to burn his clothes, not in response to specific situations, but as a generalized behavior to alleviate anxiety. The earlier connection with reality simply made it easier for him to rationalize his behavior.

Compulsive behaviors are irrational or *superstitious* coping strategies. Although they reduce the individual's obsessional anxieties, they do nothing meaningful to avert the feared consequences. Such behaviors not only serve no useful purpose, but they can become the focal point of a person's entire existence. In such cases, the person's fear becomes a secondary problem. The primary problem is the compulsive behavior, which is often bizarre, sometimes destructive, and always nonadaptive. Professional help is nearly always required to break the cycle of obsession followed by compulsion.

THE OBSESSIVE-COMPULSIVE LOOP

Figure 9-1 is the familiar learning cycle applied to obsessive-compulsive behaviors. It begins with a person experiencing a fear, usually of something that cannot be directly confronted. The fear is followed by a particular behavior. If the behavior relieves the anxiety, then the next time the fear occurs, the person is likely to repeat the same behavior. Learning by reward is taking place, and, with each repetition of obsession, compulsion, and anxiety reduction, the associative link becomes stronger. Unless the loop is broken, the frequency and intensity of the obsession is likely to escalate. Therefore, a correspondingly greater amount of time must be devoted to the compulsive behavior.

Because compulsive behaviors bear no clear-cut relationship to the obsessions they serve, the question naturally arises, How do compulsive behaviors start in the first place? Compulsive behaviors may occur from an inability to discriminate what makes one situation different from an-

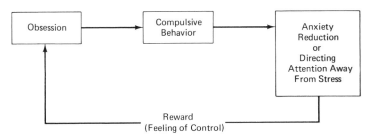

Figure 9-1. The learning cycle applied to obsessive-compulsive behavior.

other. As with Howard Hughes's clothes-burning ritual, compulsive behavior may be a misguided attempt to do something appropriate and useful. However, what makes clothes-burning appropriate in one case (disposing of the infected garments of a smallpox victim, for example), does not hold true in all cases. It is not a useful way to combat VD and is certainly inappropriate when no definable contamination of any kind has taken place.

Similarly, a person who fears cancer may begin to compulsively avoid hospitals. The rationalization goes like this: "People with cancer go to hospitals; by avoiding people with cancer, I reduce the chances of getting it myself; therefore, I should avoid hospitals." The obsessive-compulsive conveniently ignores all the relevant features that make the argument invalid. Cancer is not caused by person-to-person contact; even contagious diseases (of which cancer is not one) are nearly always adequately contained in hospitals today by careful quarantine and sanitary procedures. Driving or walking past hospitals simply does not expose a person to any more germs, viruses, and other microorganisms than does walking by a barbershop, for example, or any other place. All factors that discriminate sensible disease-avoidance procedures are ignored by the obsessive-compulsive. Moreover, for the obsessive-compulsive who reasons that hospitals must be shunned, a fifteen-minute trip from home to work may be transformed into a wildly circuitous three-hour journey.

Obsessive-compulsive behavior may also be initiated by an unfortunate chance pairing of events. This type of learning experience is illustrated in an experiment conducted by Harvard psychologist, B.F. Skinner.

Skinner was using a mechanical feeding device designed to reward a pigeon with a kernel of corn when the feeding bar was pecked under certain conditions. At one point, the device jammed and began to supply corn continuously. Skinner noted that, when this happened, the pigeon had been strutting about in more or less random circles. The pigeon made short work of the bonanza. Subsequently, Skinner noted that the pigeon was more likely to try to coax food from the device by walking about in random circles than by pecking the feeder bar as it had learned earlier. The chance pairing of a behavior (walking in random circles) with a reward had forged a strong link. Skinner realized that he had observed the creation of a superstition in an animal.

The same model of chance learning applies to compulsive behavior. A person sitting in an airplane and obsessed with fear of dying begins to touch himself nervously—scratching an ear, rubbing a finger under his nose, stroking his chin. For any number of reasons, the obsession is momentarily interrupted: perhaps the person becomes distracted from the thought of death long enough to focus on the ''here and now'' sensation of the hand on the ear. With the obsession interrupted, anxiety drops. The scratching, rubbing, stroking behavior is thus reinforced and is likely to be invoked the next time the obsessive thought arises.

Speculations about what causes people to adopt compulsive behaviors are rather academic. Treatment does not require a knowledge of original causes. The important point to note is that such behaviors can be accounted for in terms of unfortunate learning experiences and are by no means symptoms of insanity or psychotic behavior. However, if allowed to expand, deeper problems can result.

MAINTENANCE OF COMPULSIVE BEHAVIOR

Learning theory also appears capable of explaining why compulsive behaviors persist, even though they are nonadaptive. Each cycle of the obsessive-compulsive loop carries with it a prediction that takes this general form: *I fear that something dreadful will happen to me. However, if I behave in a certain way (wash my hands, make a particular gesture, say certain words), I will be safe.* Since the feared consequences of the obsession never happen, the prediction is always verified. The obsessive-compulsive almost never tests the inverse of the hypothesis to see what would happen if the compulsive behavior were *not* carried out. If he does, he meets with such anxiety that he resorts to the compulsive behavior.

The fallacy of this line of nonreasoning is made obvious by the apocryphal story of the man who kept tigers away from his Manhattan penthouse by waving his arms and crying, "Shoo!" "Do you really think that works?" asked an incredulous friend. The man replied smugly, "You don't see any tigers, do you?"

Interestingly, the people whose lives eventually become most controlled by compulsive behavior are those who can be the most indulgent of their obsessions and compulsions. Surrounded by people who were well paid to humor his eccentricities, Howard Hughes was uniquely able to carry out his compulsions because of his enormous wealth. With less money, he would have had to think twice about burning up his entire wardrobe on whim. Because he could indulge every compulsion, Hughes constructed more and more elaborate defenses until he became virtually sealed off from everything in the world except the germs he feared most. For all his wealth, power, eccentricities, and outlandish compulsions, however, the air he breathed, the food he ate, and the clothes he wore almost certainly contained not one less germ than if he had lived the life of a normal, sociable human being.

Sometimes, an obsessive-compulsive individual is forced to give up a particular behavior or to seek professional help because his or her environment is less permissive of the compulsive behaviors. A person who must dress a dozen different times each morning, making sure each button is done just so and each shoelace tied just right, may be forced to abandon the ritual if he or she is faced with getting to work on time and earning a living. Compulsions grow where the conditions are most suitable.

SUPERSTITIONS AS COMPULSIVE BEHAVIOR

"Step on a crack, break your mother's back," goes a children's rhyme. "Don't walk under a ladder," and "It's bad luck if a black cat crosses your path," warn two old sayings. While most people don't take these superstitions seriously, nonetheless a surprising number do heed such advice. And so, they take some pains to avoid cracks in the sidewalk, ladders, black cats, broken mirrors, the number thirteen, spilled salt, cross-eyed people, and looking at a new moon through the branches of a tree. When asked why they do so, a good many of these people sheepishly reply, "Well, it can't hurt."

Superstition is simply another form of obsessive-compulsive behavior, one that is often shared by many members of society. A fear of bad luck, for example, is followed by a behavioral response that has usually been consciously learned, such as avoiding black cats. If, as nearly always happens, no bad luck follows, the superstitious behavior is rewarded. The prediction is verified: "If I change directions so that black cats don't cross my path, nothing bad will happen." And lo and behold, nothing usually does.

However, almost everyone knows someone (or someone who knows someone) who failed to heed the warning and shortly thereafter suffered grievous bad luck. And, although isolated instances of black-cat sightings followed by accidents are no more than the chance pairing of a behavior and a consequence (à la Skinner and his pigeon), for some people they serve as powerful confirmations of superstitious beliefs.

Superstition and fear are sometimes components of religious practices. Fear of punishment by an offended deity may motivate the use of certain gestures, spoken phrases, and ritualistic behaviors. Even among religious people, there is likely to be little agreement about what separates superstitious nonsense from religious behavior. For instance, the agnostic may view all those who pray as superstitious. On the other hand, some of those who pray consider their own behavior religious, but contend that those who employ beads, relics, and statues are superstitious. And even many of those who agree on prayers, beads, and other symbols may draw the line when it comes to shaking a tambourine and chanting "Hare Krishna" all day.

Superstitious behaviors can be relatively harmless. However, like most actions carried to extremes, they can also be destructive. Rooted in fear, superstitious behaviors, like compulsive behaviors, are no alternative to rational and adaptive methods of coping with an anxiety-provoking world.

TREATMENT OF OBSESSIVE-COMPULSIVE BEHAVIOR

According to conventional psychoanalytic theory, obsessive-compulsive individuals are considered to be on the verge of psychosis. Treatment through psychoanalysis is slow and tedious, with the therapist taking great care not to upset the delicate balance that is supposedly being maintained through the compulsive behavior. Deprived of the compulsive behavior, so the theory goes, the obsessive-compulsive individual is in danger of tumbling into complete psychosis.

Modern research has shown that this is simply not so. Denied the ability to carry out compulsive behavior, a patient may become temporarily destructive, violent, and abusive in the extreme—but not psychotic. One reason that obsessive-compulsive behavior may have been considered nearly psychotic is because compulsive individuals will go to great lengths to maintain their behaviors. So strong is their desire to carry out the compulsive behavior that they can intimidate even experienced therapists with threats of "going crazy," "tearing the room apart," or "killing myself," if their ability to carry out the compulsion is hindered.

Behavior therapy uses a technique called *response prevention* to treat obsessive-compulsives. The technique can only be carried out in highly controlled conditions under the guidance of an experienced professional therapist. *Under no circumstances should the treatment be attempted in any other way.*

Quite simply, response prevention involves outside intervention between the obsession and the compulsive behavior that follows—that is, the patient is physically restrained from carrying out the compulsive behavior. In one such case, a female patient—obsessed about germs so that whenever she touched food, particularly raw meat, she would spend long periods scrubbing her hands—was given the task of making meatballs. After a few minutes of forming the meat into balls, she became overwhelmed by the need to wash her hands. When she was not allowed to carry out her compulsion, she became angry and began to make loud, violent threats. This behavior continued for several hours. A therapist was with her constantly to lend moral support in between her periods of raging. When it was all over, the strong link between obsessive fears and compulsive handwashing had been successfully broken.

This method of treatment is still not extremely common, for it requires that the patient be institutionalized during treatment; in addition not many places are equipped to handle such problems. Also, the treatment is quite uncomfortable and unpleasant so that even those who strongly wish to be rid of their compulsive behaviors are hesitant to undergo the therapy.

Another technique that has been used successfully is called *graduated response prevention.* This treatment aims toward the same goal as *total response prevention,* but does not try to break the association all at once. Instead, the patient attempts to build a time delay into the obsession-compulsion loop. When the compulsion arises, the patient sets a timer, waits until an agreed-upon time has passed, and then carries out the compulsive behavior. At first, the time delay is quite small, no more than fifteen or twenty seconds. Gradually, the time is increased.

The rationale for graduated response prevention therapy is simply that learning by reinforcement occurs only when the reinforcement (anxiety reduction in this case) closely follows the triggering stimulus (the obsession). As the reinforcement gets further away in time, it is greatly weakened. When this therapy is successful, the patient eventually reaches a point at which it is sometimes possible to skip compulsive episodes occasionally, and later with more frequency, until the associative link is finally broken for good. All the while, the therapist can be working with the patient to develop rational and meaningful coping strategies to reduce any obsessional anxieties that still persist.

10.
FEAR OF
HEALTH CARE

Fear of going to a physician or dentist should be considered for three reasons. First, just about everyone at some time has experienced a fear of health-care delivery. Second, the range of strategies for consciously coping with these fears illustrates concretely how the methods we have discussed can be combined to treat complex fears. Third, these fears can profoundly affect people's lives, not only by limiting their self-determination, but by actually preventing them from pursuing a rational course of action essential to their own well-being.

The delivery of health care does inflict some pain and discomfort, often involving being stuck with needles, probed in sensitive areas, and having metal instruments placed on our skin, in our ears, and up our noses. To fear pain is both sensible and adaptive, but to endanger you health for the sake of avoiding relatively minor unpleasantries is neither rational nor adaptive. Indeed, by avoiding the minor discomforts that go with regular checkups, you risk incurring far greater pain somewhere down the road. Preventive medicine is nearly always less painful than restorative medicine.

Unfortunately, unpleasant childhood experiences with doctors and dentists tend to be remembered forever. Well-meaning parents or doctors are sometimes guilty of using misleading tactics to keep a child from being afraid. Thus, before giving an injection, a doctor might say, "This won't hurt a bit." The child, unconvinced, watches the approaching needle, focusing on the point where it pierces the skin. The shot may not be painful, but the concentrated attention and the child's expectations may magnify the sensation until it *seems* like pain. Moreover, if the child flinches unexpectedly or tenses his muscles, genuine pain may result. In any case, the child who feels pain, after being told he won't be hurt, is not likely to be as trusting the next time. A broken trust thus becomes the basis for a later fear.

Another problem centers on dealing with physicians and dentists as authority figures. Children are sometimes told, "Do just what the nice doctor says. Don't argue. It's for your own good." This pattern of behavior carried uncritically into adult life, can create a sense of powerlessness and give rise to a lack of assertiveness in dealing with health-care authorities.

Most physicians and dentists today agree that patients have the right to know the results of a diagnosis, the benefits and drawbacks of a recommended therapy or medication, and the cost, in advance, of treatment. But patients who become timid and anxious around a medical authority figure may be afraid to ask for this information. They may fear appearing stupid, acting inappropriately, or showing their fear. In addition, many people are afraid that doctors or dentists may shame them by treating them as children or by making degrading remarks ("You have terrible teeth. Don't you ever brush?").

Fear of visiting the dentist is among the most common and deep-seated of all fears. First of all, the patient is awake while being treated by a dentist. In addition, even the most gentle dentist may cause some discomfort, although high-speed drills and modern anesthetics have almost eliminated the major sources of pain. Also, for many people, having someone poke around in their mouths is more than a trivial invasion of the body. Finally, years ago, dentists had little or no formal training and perhaps did not understand their potential for creating fear. Even today, some dentists focus more on the technical aspects of dentistry than on the patient's comfort. Recent studies have shown that nearly two-thirds of all Americans have mild to severe apprehension about dental care. In response to this, all major dental schools now teach psychological techniques of patient management.

In this chapter, we relate a case history of dentist fear as treated by a therapist; much of the subsequent discussion is also applicable to health-care fears in general. In addition, many of the behavioral techniques employed by the therapist in this account can be effectively adapted to work in a program of self-help.

A CASE HISTORY OF DENTAL FEAR

Mr. McR., a busy and successful lawyer, knew that he needed dental work. He had noticed that one tooth had become sensitive to hot and cold, a condition that was growing worse and that sometimes caused considerable pain. Even so, Mr. McR. had been able to convince himself that his crowded schedule did not permit time for a visit to the dentist. A couple of times he had his secretary make an appointment for him, but he always cancelled at the last minute—for business reasons. As the toothaches grew more frequent and more painful, he was forced to face the truth: he was afraid to go to the dentist. Moreover, his fear was so strong that, even when faced with the reality of certain pain if he did not go, he could not bring himself to keep an appointment.

Convinced that he needed help, he contacted a psychologist and sheepishly confessed his problem.

The therapist learned at the first interview that Mr. McR.'s fears were not limited to any one aspect of dental practice—they ranged over just about every facet of dentistry from start to finish. The normally confident and assertive Mr. McR. felt like a child when dealing with a dentist. He was afraid to ask questions. He feared that either the pain would be overwhelming or that his response to it would be so great as to make him look a complete idiot. He was frightened by needles, drills, probes, and anything else that a dentist might stick in his mouth. And, although Mr. McR. earned a good salary, he was nonetheless anxious about incurring a large dental bill.

The therapist persuaded Mr. McR. to enlist the cooperation of a competent dentist who would be willing to provide the support necessary to overcome a fear problem. He was also given a homework assignment: to write out what he might say to explain his fear to a dentist. He was given these guidelines: Explain (1) that you have a fear problem and need special help, (2) that you require a preliminary visit to discuss procedures before any work is done, (3) that you expect the dentist to be an active partner in helping you deal with the fear, and (4) that you require an estimate of the cost of any work to be done.

At the next session, a week later, the therapist played the role of a dentist, and Mr. McR. practiced his presentation. Based on this rehearsal Mr. McR. discovered better ways of expressing himself to make his case clearer and stronger. He also gained confidence in his ability to ask questions and evaluate the answers. He then called several dentists and selected one who not only was particularly sympathetic to the problem but who had received special training in dealing with fearful patients as well. (Such dentists are becoming increasingly common as the dental profession works to improve both its practices and its image with the public.) The therapist followed up with a telephone call to the dentist in which they discussed the cooperative approach that would be used.

During the next several sessions with the therapist, Mr. McR. was introduced to relaxation techniques and thought-stopping. At the same time, he was working with the therapist's guidance to develop a fear hierarchy that listed the total experience of visiting the dentist in gradual steps ranging from its least fearful to most fearful aspects. When completed, the hierarchy read as follows:

1. Making an appointment with the dentist.
2. Driving to the dentist's office.
3. Riding up the elevator to the office.
4. Walking into the waiting room.
5. Giving name to the receptionist.
6. Sitting down and waiting.
7. Being called into the dentist's office.
8. Seeing the instrument console and the chair.
9. Sitting in the chair.
10. Having a bib fastened around the neck.
11. The dentist saying, "Open up."
12. The dentist putting a mirror and probe into the mouth.
13. Feeling the probe touching the teeth and gums.
14. Having the teeth scaled.
15. Being told that there are cavities that need attention.
16. Having an anesthetic gel applied to the gum in preparation for an injection.
17. Having an injection of novocaine to numb the nerves around a tooth.
18. Seeing the dentist approach with the drill.

19. Hearing the sound of the drill.
20. Feeling the drill against the tooth.
21. Experiencing temporary pain as the drill strikes a sensitive spot.
22. Having a tooth extracted.

Mr. McR. was instructed to imagine these scenes one at a time and to check his SUD rating after each step. If the reading was below 10, he was to continue. If not, he was to stop and do relaxation exercises until the level dropped to 10 or below, and then he was to back up one step and begin again.

He had little trouble working through the hierarchy in fantasy. Within two weeks, he could imagine each step without going above a SUD rating of 10. At that point, the therapist contacted the dentist and arranged for Mr. McR. to begin working through the hierarchy in reality. The patient was warned that he would feel more anxious than when merely imagining the procedures.

On a Monday morning, rested from the weekend, Mr. McR. made his first visit to the dentist's office. He knew that no dental work would be performed that day. It was a dry run to put into practice the new coping strategies of relaxation that he had learned. To ensure the best chance for success, he went through a relaxation session before leaving the house. When he got into his car to drive to the dentist's office, he was at a very comfortable 10 on the SUD scale. Having been instructed to monitor his SUD ratings at each step, he realized when he arrived in the waiting room that he had jumped from a 15, which he experienced in the elevator (step 3), to nearly 30. However, ten minutes of relaxation exercises (described in Chapter 4) in the waiting room and a brief run-through of the guided imagery lowered the SUD rating to 10. He later commented to the therapist that step 6, waiting to be called into the dentist's office, had always been a period of particularly intense anxiety and discomfort. Therefore, he was pleased to discover that this same situation could be turned to his advantage, when used, not as a time to obsess about what was coming, but rather to increase relaxation and prepare for the next, and admittedly more difficult, steps.

In reviewing his initial dental visit with the therapist, Mr. McR. said he had had no difficulty with steps 7 and 8. Even step 9, actually sitting in the chair, had resulted in only a small increase in his self-determined SUD rating. He explained that he thought the smallness of the increase was due primarily to his knowing that no work would be done that day. However, he reported that his anxiety had increased greatly while he sat in the chair and began to mentally rehearse the remaining steps in the hierarchy, particularly step 13, feeling the probe touch the gum. In addition, he had not been able to progress in imagination through step 17, receiving an injection of novocaine.

Mr. McR.'s difficulty at steps 13 and 17 alerted the therapist to his need for some additional desensitization. First, some dental instruments were spread out in front of the patient, who was instructed to relax, which he did with no problem. Next, he was asked to pick up the instruments, hold them, and look at them. Then, the relaxation procedure was repeated. For the next step, Mr. McR. was told to place a probe in his mouth and gently touch it to his own gums. This he did with ease. Next, the therapist played the role of the dentist, and Mr. McR. practiced relaxation techniques while the therapist gently inserted the probe in Mr. McR.'s mouth and touched it to his teeth and gums. After three such trials, Mr. McR. had dropped his SUD level from above 30 to a fairly calm 15.

One full session was devoted to systematic desensitization

toward hypodermic needles. The session began with Mr. McR. viewing the disassembled needle from a distance. In much the same way as he learned to approach the dental probes, he was gradually introduced to the needle: first, in pieces and at a distance; then, still in pieces but close up; next, by holding the pieces. Whenever the SUD level rose, he stopped, did relaxation exercises, and then started again when the level was low enough. The therapist, again playing the part of the dentist, inserted a toothpick in the hypodermic syringe and gradually brought it closer and closer to Mr. McR. until he was able to remain relaxed even with the wooden tip touching his gum. Finally, the procedure was repeated with the actual needle in place. Several tries were required for Mr. McR. to control the steep SUD increase; however, by the end of a one-hour session, he had reduced his tension to 15 and felt comfortable enough with the procedure to practice it in his own home.

With the mutual agreement of Mr. McR., his therapist, and the dentist, an actual working visit to the dentist was arranged. The visit was to involve only an initial inspection and cleaning. Mr. McR. was instructed to think of the visit in exactly the same way as he had approached the practice session. Indeed, there was no difference, because Mr. McR. could stop the treatment at any time he chose. In fact, Mr. McR. had been specifically instructed to stop the procedures any time his SUD level went above 20.

The initial meeting was an unqualified success. Twice during the cleaning period Mr. McR. asked the dentist to stop while he composed himself. Each time, he was able to resume undergoing the cleaning. To celebrate the success of the visit, Mr. McR. and his wife ate at their favorite seafood restaurant that night and went to a movie.

Unfortunately, the second visit did not go so well. The dentist had discovered that several of Mr. McR.'s teeth were in need of fillings and that one had gone without attention for so long that it probably would have to be removed. Mr. McR. received the bad news stoically, and dutifully made an appointment to have the first cavities filled. At the therapist's suggestion, Mr. McR. asked that only two minor cavities be filled and that the larger ones and the extraction be put off to a later visit. By pacing the visits in this way, Mr. McR. greatly increased his chances for success. The dentist readily agreed to the arrangement.

The second visit fell on a Thursday afternoon. It had been a hectic week for Mr. McR. as he prepared for an approaching court case, and he was working with his client right up to the moment that he had to leave for his appointment. Traffic was worse than usual, and he arrived only minutes before his appointment.

When the dentist asked him to step into the office, Mr. McR. knew that he was well above the 20 level on the SUD scale, but he didn't want to backslide after having made such good progress up until that time. He assumed that he would relax once he got into the chair. But he didn't. Instead of concentrating on relaxing, he grew more anxious over his desire to get the job over with. Sensing his anxiety, the dentist asked him if he needed time to calm down. Mr. McR. assured him bravely that everything was fine. Then the drill started. Mr. McR. began to sweat. His heart was pounding, and his mouth became so dry that he was afraid he would choke. Finally, he called off the session. It was several days before he could bring himself to call the therapist and report his failure.

As the therapist pointed out, Mr. McR. had no reason to brand himself a failure. He had not necessarily used the best judgment in trying to brave his way through the session, but his decision not to go through with it that particular day was in fact something of a victory. Mr. McR. had been assertive enough to admit, "No, I can't handle it today." In so doing, he had made it easier to go back the next time. Had he forced himself to stick it out at that session, the bad experience might have been enough to keep him away from the dentist until his teeth were beyond saving.

Mr. McR. agreed to try another visit. This time, he scheduled it for a Monday, first thing in the morning. Also, the therapist gave him a cassette tape on which were recorded twenty minutes of the sound of a dentist's drill. Mr. McR. was to practice relaxation with the drill sound going, just to ensure that his one bad experience with the drill had not inadvertently set in motion a pattern of associative learning that could work to his disadvantage.

The next visit went well. Rested, and consciously focused on maintaining relaxation, Mr. McR. had no difficulties. Subsequent visits became increasingly easier as he became both more adept at relaxation and more comfortable knowing what he would actually be experiencing. Although some of the worst cavities were saved until last, by the time the dentist began to treat them, Mr. McR.'s abilities to remain calm were equal to the task.

The tooth extraction was saved for the last visit, prior to which Mr. McR. paid a final visit to the therapist. Together, they reviewed the fundamentals of relaxing. In addition, the therapist stressed the importance of thought-stopping. If Mr. McR. allowed himself to dwell on the thought of the pain of having a tooth pulled, it would make it harder for him to relax. Thus, he was instructed to actively try to stop such thoughts with thought-stopping techniques. Also, it was important to have the program of dental care end on a satisfactory note in order to encourage Mr. McR. to follow up with a program of preventive treatment that would reduce the need for future restorative work.

Because Mr. McR. expressed some fear of gagging when

he was forced to keep his mouth open wide with instruments inside, the therapist suggested a simple procedure. It involved placing the tip of the tongue against the lower front teeth and then closing off the airway to the oral cavity with the base of the tongue. When done properly, Mr. McR. could hum through his nose, even with his mouth wide open. The procedure accomplished three things: it got the tongue out of the way so the dentist could work in the mouth; it sealed off the throat from saliva or blood; and it allowed Mr. McR. to breathe through his nose so that he wouldn't inhale anything that could cause him to choke or gag.

SUMMARY

The techniques that we have described have worked, singularly and in combination, for many people with fears of dentists and physicians. In addition, hypnosis and the use of nitrous oxide are also being successfully applied to alleviate such phobias. The old days of false assurances and degrading statements are gone from modern dentistry.

The person using relaxation and desensitization techniques to overcome fears of doctors and dentists should bear in mind the following points:

- *Assertion is essential.* Tell the doctor that you are dealing with a fear problem and that you expect help with it. If you get a fast brush-off or a parental just-leave-everything-to-me-and-don't-worry, find another doctor. Ask questions. Listen to the answers, and understand them. If you get a response of "It's all too complicated for you," you probably have the wrong doctor.
- *A visit to a doctor or dentist should be a learning experience.* If you are basically healthy, you should learn something during such a visit about staying that way. If

you have a medical problem, you need to learn what to do, to consider alternatives, and to make sound decisions with the doctor's help. You won't learn without asking questions. However, questions won't help if you don't press for understandable answers.

● *Remember, physicians and dentists are people whose job is providing services for you.* You have a right to know what the service does and does not include, how much it will cost, and what the risks are. After all, it's your body and your health.

● *Scheduling your visits is important.* If you are having extensive treatment, try to have the easier, least painful sessions first. Build up to the harder session gradually, and thus give your confidence a chance to grow. Try to schedule visits on nonstressful days, or at times when you will be relaxed, rested, and best able to cope. Piling stress on top of stress invites failure and creates negative learning situations that make the next visit more difficult.

● *Try to relax in the actual situation—the waiting room, the dentist's chair, etc.* Instruct your physician or dentist in the techniques you are using to cope. This can be particularly important in overcoming fears.

● *Be alert to specific fears, such as a fear of needles or other instruments.* Sometimes, these fears influence the patient's whole attitude toward health care, and, by specific desensitization techniques, they can be overcome. Also, by being aware of these specific fears, the doctor may be able to work around them until your confidence allows you to handle the situation more easily.

Finally, ignorance is not bliss. Ignorance is ignorance, pure and simple. When it comes to your health, what you *don't* know can hurt you.

11.
SEXUAL FEARS

The sexual responses of men and women are determined and influenced by a great many factors—physiological, cultural, educational, situational, and psychological. These, as well as other factors, contribute to what we feel, think, and do in relation to the whole complex topic of human sexuality.

For many reasons, sexual enjoyment and fulfillment can be impaired. Fears associated with sex and sexual practices are extremely common, although they are by no means the only reasons why people fail to achieve satisfactory sex lives. Sexual fears exact their toll of human suffering in several ways. Such fears can prevent any true intimacy from ever developing between individuals. They can interfere with the enjoyment and pleasure that sex offers. And, in many cases, fear can make the sexual act impossible. The bodily responses associated with fear are incompatible with the responses required for sexual activity. If fear is telling the body to get ready to fight or run, conscious willpower alone cannot produce an erection, lubricate the walls of the vagina, or create a mental state conducive to achieving orgasm.

Three approaches to sexual problems make up the mainstream of today's psychotherapy. The first of these, *psy-*

choanalysis, derives from the work of Freud and his disciples. Freudian theory contends that sexual problems are the result of unconscious sexual desire for one's parents, which results in castration fears, oedipal complexes, fixation upon father figures, and a host of other neuroses. Treatment, which is typically prolonged, is aimed at bringing the conflicts up to a conscious level. The theory assumes that conscious scrutiny of one's own conflicts will lead to a resolution of the problem.

The second technique in current use focuses on inappropriate or destructive interactions between two people as the root of certain sexual problems. *Marital counseling* (or *couple's counseling,* as it is called) attacks sexual problems within the context of interpersonal relationships. What two people say and don't say, what they do and don't do, how they act and react are the data for analyzing sexual difficulties and attempting to construct a solution.

The third approach, which is behavioral, is known as *direct sexual therapy.* It draws upon the same basic theory that we have relied upon in our discussion of fear. Starting from a foundation of learning theory, behavioral psychologists view certain sexual disorders as problems of behavior. Like other forms of behavior, sexual behaviors are learned. Therefore, they are subject to change by *classical conditioning* (learning by association) and *reinforcement* (learning by rewards). Behavioral treatments, which concentrate on relieving the patient of the symptoms of a particular problem, offer more immediate relief than do other types of therapy. When these techniques are effective, they can help to decrease general anxiety levels and thereby increase the likelihood of successful treatment of any related problems.

The three approaches outlined here are not mutually exclusive. Sexual problems rooted in childhood conflict or interpersonal discord can sometimes be improved by eliminating the immediate symptoms, which are amenable to behavioral therapies. The problems that can be most readily treated through behavioral techniques are sometimes considered to be relatively superficial. However, the onset of such problems can aggravate more deep-seated issues that might never have surfaced in the absence of the immediate, or so-called superficial, problem. Adequate treatment of sexual problems may require some aspects of each type of therapy.

Occasionally, sexual fears instilled in childhood and nurtured in adolescence reach their peak in adult life. They may become generalized to cover a whole range of attitudes toward sex. Thus, changing any single aspect of behavior may be ineffective in treating such problems. Fears that permeate many different aspects of an individual's behavior may become deeply entrenched and protected through elaborate rationalizations and an almost inpenetrable maze of defense mechanisms. Such far-ranging fears essentially affect the entire personality; it is beyond the scope of this chapter to consider them.

We focus here on simpler, more immediate types of sexual fears—those that arise from rather specific types of learning situations. The techniques that we have presented in earlier chapters are adaptable to these simpler fears and sexual problems. We explain here how these techniques can be applied to problems of performance anxiety, fear of rejection, and sexual inhibitions arising out of fear.

PERFORMANCE ANXIETY

A man who approaches lovemaking afraid that he may fail to achieve an erection is working on a self-fulfilling prophecy. His apprehension may cause the very event he fears: failure to get an erection. A woman who fears that she will not be able to please her partner or to reach orgasm is already well on the way to failure on both counts. For both men and women, anxiety over sexual performance can lead to failure to perform at all.

Figure 11-1 illustrates how the preceding situation is a classic example of learning by association.

Fear of failure creates anxiety. The greater the anxiety, the less the likelihood of being able to perform adequately. Since the autonomic nervous system is incapable of preparing the body for sex and at the same time maintaining high levels of anxiety, the individual's sexual abilities are diminished by fear. The more the ability diminishes, the greater the anxiety, until at last, failure occurs—unless the loop is broken in some way. Each failure creates negative expectations that become associated with the individual's ability to perform sexually. Ironically enough, as failure occurs, the need for perfection, may increase.

What causes a person with healthy sexual desires to get to the crucial point of initiating intercourse only to be thwarted by performance anxiety? The most common reason is an obsession with what might happen, instead of focusing on what is in fact happening. For example, as John and Marcia prepare to make love, they become aroused. Certain physiological changes take place in their bodies. The immediate sights, sounds, smells, tastes, and tactile sensations that

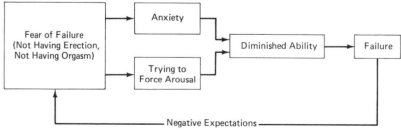

Figure 11-1. An example of learning by association applied to sexual fears.

they experience are all cooperating to make intercourse possible and pleasurable. Then, inexplicably, the problem begins. John finds himself thinking, not of how pleasant all this is, but rather, "Will I be able to keep this erection? Will I last long enough to satisfy her? Will I be deft and suave, or clumsy and fumbling?" Meanwhile, Marcia, has stepped outside of her own passion long enough to wonder, "Should I move and let him know I enjoy it once he is in me, or should I be passive and lie still? Will I reach orgasm? Will he be disappointed with me if I don't reach a climax?" The particular questions in John's and Marcia's minds are anxiety-provoking; moreover, the very act of asking any question whose answer is not certain is anxiety-provoking in itself. Unless this scenario is straightened out right away, John and Marcia will probably wind up watching the late show or going out for ice cream—both of them angry and frustrated, and neither quite sure just what happened to dampen the tenderness and passion that each had felt but had been unable to consummate.

That such obsessive thoughts are common is not surprising, given the attitudes toward sex that prevail in our society and the circumstances under which sexual behavior is frequently learned. For instance, John and Marcia's experience may have begun in a parked car, a situation that presents the constant possibility of discovery and the subsequent humiliation at being found (gasp!) in the act of making love. Vigilance, which is not very compatible with relaxation, is thus a prerequisite. Although youthful ardor may be equal to the challenge *(Amor vincit omnia),* watchful anxious behavior carried into later life can lead to problems.

Part of the problem in performance anxiety may simply be the failure to discriminate between behaviors that are appropriate in one situation and not another. Anxiety may well be appropriate in the parked-car scenario. However, the seclusion of a bedroom (you probably should lock the doors) is altogether different.

Even when conscious discrimination takes place, however, a difficulty may remain. The anxiety connected with making love in a parked car can transfer to other situations. Through repeated associations of anxiety and sexual intercourse, the body is conditioned to respond as if it believed, in effect, "You can't have one without the other." It may not be possible to simply "switch off" such somatically conditioned components of sexual behavior. What may be required is a learning program that reconditions the brain and body (particularly the autonomic nervous system) to develop new responses, new expectations, and new forms of sexual behavior.

Performance anxieties can sometimes be alleviated by relaxation techniques. The relaxation, while not focused on a specific fear, may serve to lower the general anxiety levels. Relaxation, coupled with thought-stopping and assertive techniques, is effective in overcoming the obsessional aspects of performance anxiety. However, instead of using television or a book to distract the mind from obsessions, as discussed in Chapter 7, the patient concentrates on the "here and now" experience of sexual arousal. Lowered anxiety levels enable a person to become aware of subtle erotic cues that may be lost in a state of anxiety. By being able to sense the early signs of arousal, a man may receive the necessary encouragement to expect and complete a successful sexual encounter. Similarly, a woman with a lowered state of anxiety may become sufficiently aware of the pleasant sensations in her body so that she is not distracted by concerns of how well she will do. With the stage set for a successful performance, a new group of expectations and behaviors may be learned.

Another technique used in overcoming performance anxiety is *non-demand pleasuring*. This involves the removal of any threat, real or imagined, that is implied by a perceived demand for sexual intercourse. The problem is illustrated in Figure 11-2.

As with other types of fear, avoidance behavior may be adopted as a coping technique. The sexual desires of the mate are perceived as demands (which, in some cases, may *be* demands), and the demand fuels the anxiety, which serves only to increase the fear.

In non-demand pleasuring, the therapist instructs the couple to choose an appropriately private and secluded time and then to engage in petting, stroking, kissing, masturbation to orgasm, and any other form of mutually acceptable amorous attention—but *not* to attempt sexual intercourse. For couples undergoing this therapy, the demand component of Figure 11-2 is removed. The net effect is to decrease anxiety, thereby making erection possible. (It also teaches each partner that the responsibility for arousal is a shared one.) Repeated achievement of an erection during non-demand play sessions builds a new set of expectations: namely, that erection will occur. Therefore, fear of impotence is usually diminished by the repeated experience of erection. One sex therapist reports that, in many of the cases he has treated in this way, the couple reaches a point when they spontaneously decide to ignore the therapist's instructions and to engage in sex. Successful and regular disobedience constitutes a solution to their problem.

One other aspect of relaxation therapy should be men-

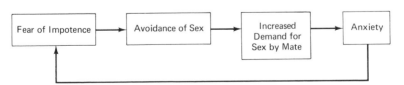

Figure 11-2.The learning cycle applied to fear of impotence.

tioned here—the "letting-go effect." People who cannot relax tend to believe that they must constantly be controlling their environment, that a letdown in vigilance invites disaster. Sexual fulfillment, however, requires a reasonably high degree of abandon, since there is an unquestionable vulnerability for people engaged in sex. Both are naked and in awkward or defenseless positions. At the moment of orgasm, there is even something of a momentary loss of contact with one's surroundings. Afterward, there may be a sensation of pleasant fatigue, a lack of inclination to do anything but lie quiet and still, perhaps to sleep. Anxiety tells us that each of these is a "no-no." Relaxation exercises, on the other hand, are aimed at teaching us to trust our bodies, to discover that bad things do not happen when we "let go." Indeed, very good things happen. We feel better, we think better, we learn better, and we perform better. Not surprisingly, a number of people who have successfully used relaxation techniques to treat nonsexual fears report an increase in sexual desire and an improved sex life.

FEAR OF REJECTION

Fear of rejection is not a specific sexual fear. However, it may play a significant role in sexual behavior, operating under the guise of timidity, shyness, or social ineptitude. Stated simply, a person who fears rejection enough to avoid social contacts and relationships will have limited opportunities for sexual fulfillment.

Ralph sits in a singles' bar night after night, sipping a manhattan and hoping to meet Ms. Right. Unfortunately, he fears rejection so much that he usually can't bring himself to start a conversation. When he does muster up the courage to speak to a candidate for Ms. Right, he is nervous, ill at ease—and definitely not cool. Moreover, he expects his attempts to fail, and so naturally they do. Since Ralph never makes a favorable first impression, romance hasn't got a chance. And so, these days, his barroom conversations are pretty much limited to ordering another drink from the bartender.

People who fear rejection often have a rigid view of the world that confuses one aspect of behavior with the total person. Their attitude says, in effect, "This is the way *I* behave. Take it or leave it." Such people mistake rejection of any one form of behavior for rejection of the total person.

If Ralph were to list the way he acts in various social situations, he would discover that he has a whole repertoire of behaviors that he employs on various occasions. His list might read like this:

Singles' Bar Situations	*With Close Friends*
Uncomfortable	At ease
Gruff	Open
Quiet	Fun-loving
Unsure	

At Work	*Recreational Situations*
Conscientious	Intense
Competent	Highly competitive
	Poor loser

Ralph could help himself by changing the way he views himself and by discarding his incorrect model of reality. You are *not* your behavior. Your behavior is something that you emit. You can change your behavior, and behaviors do change through experience and practice. Ralph needs to start by realizing that the rejection of his singles' bar behavior is not the same as the rejection of him as a person. Overcoming a fear of rejection may entail (1) admitting that certain forms of behavior are not producing the desired results, (2) discarding unproductive or destructive behaviors, and (3) adopting new ones designed to serve some desired end.

Relaxation can also help play a role in overcoming rejection fears. Lower levels of anxiety make any learning task easier, including the learning of new social behaviors that enhance your ability to make a good impression. In addition, relaxation helps communication: you can think more clearly because you are concentrating on what is being said and not on whether you are doing or saying the right thing. Also, tension is communicated as much by subtle body movements as by what you say (or fail to say). Relaxation lends an air of self-assurance to your whole presence, which puts other people at ease and helps them to open up to you.

Assertion techniques are also helpful in fighting a fear of rejection. Modeling your social behavior on that of someone you consider socially adept is one of the fastest and surest ways of picking up assertive behavior. Some people resist this kind of conscious modeling: "It just isn't me," they explain. This simply indicates that they are being governed by the false model of the world in which the total personality and its myriad behaviors are confused with one single aspect of behavior.

Clearly, you want your individual behaviors to be consistent with other aspects of your life and beliefs, and you should choose your model accordingly. But to refuse to change because, "It's not me," is to persist in failure and to let your life be governed by fear.

ATTITUDES, INHIBITIONS, AND FEARS

Sex inevitably begins as a mystery. Children are exposed to various aspects of sexuality without having a context of experience in which to understand it. Just as a person blind from birth cannot really understand colors, a child prior to puberty lacks the physical equipment to understand the sexual messages being communicated by parents, peers, television, magazines, and other media. No amount of prior preparation can fully dispel the mystery—only growth, maturity, and experience can yield understanding. Moreover, fear of the unknown is common. And when the unknown is invested with such significance as sex enjoys, it is small wonder that the associated fears should be so numerous and far-reaching.

Many voyagers into this constantly unfolding unknown—sex—labor under severe handicaps. Through misinformation, inadequate education, and unrealistic moralities, attitudes are developed that have little connection to reality. Little girls are taught that kissing leads to pregnancy. Little boys are told that masturbation will ruin their health and doom them to perdition. When children are warned that "Sex talk is dirty," "Nice girls don't do things like that," and "God (and parents) punish bad little boys," it is no wonder that the roots of sexual fears sprout early and grow deep.

Attitudes beget inhibitions, and inhibitions beget rigid and narrow patterns of behavior bounded by fear. Education and communication are essential to the change of attitudes. Early education that provides facts about sex and sexual development is certainly a sounder foundation for growth than the whispered fantasies that too often pass for sex education. Education alone cannot illuminate the unknown or its imagined terrors; it can, however, make the unknown less fearful. Furthermore, by helping to shape atittudes on the basis of facts, education can present sex as the natural, healthy, joyful experience that it is, not the demon that myth would have it be.

In treating patients with sexual fears, therapists frequently encounter individuals who are literally at a loss for words when trying to discuss any aspect of sex. Verbal desensitization may be required to break the silence barrier and to provide patients with the vocabulary to discuss their bodies, sexual acts, and their feelings about sex. Sometimes, permission from an authority figure—the therapist—is all that patients need to feel free to "use certain words." Other times, relaxation exercises, together with the repetition of hearing the "forbidden words," is required. Frank, uninhibited group discussions are another useful technique in verbal desensitization. The acquisition of a vocabularly and the freedom to use it do not miraculously banish sexual fears, but it is certainly a positive first step. One sex therapist has written that trying to be adequate in lovemaking without communication is "like trying to learn target shooting blindfolded." In the difficult area of sexual fears, commmunication is not the final answer, but, without it, there can be no answers at all.

Additional Information

The Art and Science of Love, Albert Ellis, Lyle Stuart, 1960.

For Yourself: The Fulfillment of Female Sexuality, Lonnie G. Barbach, Anchor Press/Doubleday, 1976.

Human Sexual Inadequacy, William H. Masters and Virginia E. Johnson, Little, Brown, 1970.

The New Sex Therapy: Active Treatment of Sexual Dysfunctions, Helen S. Kaplan, Brunner-Mazel, 1974.

The Sensuous Person: Critique and Corrections, Albert Ellis, Lyle Stuart, 1973.

12.
FEAR OF FLYING

On a bright Sunday morning in early spring, Ted R., the flight-phobic salesman we met in Chapter 1, boarded a Pan American jetliner at Boston's Logan International Airport. The passengers who boarded with him looked like any other group of travelers, except that they were perhaps slightly more solemn and intense. As the plane roared off the runway and banked over Boston Harbor, the captain's voice crackled over the intercom system: "Congratulations, ladies and gentlemen. We are airborne." After a moment of quiet disbelief, a cheer went up from every passenger aboard. They stood up, hugged one another, and applauded. Within moments, champagne flowed freely, and toasts abounded. People roamed the aisles, talking and laughing, and even Ted was at ease and enjoying himself. It was a joyful, remarkable scene because, only a few weeks earlier, each passenger had been afraid to fly.

The plane trip was the final exercise in a program designed to transform white-knuckled flight-phobics into contented air travelers.* It consisted of ten two-hour classes held once a week for ten weeks. Classes were directed by

*The program described was developed by Dr. Forgione and conducted with Dr. Surwit.

147

professional therapists working with a group. We will focus in some detail on the structure of these classes and on the techniques that they employ because they serve as a useful model for individuals trying to overcome fears on their own. With some thought and imagination you should be able to adapt some of the ideas presented here for learning new behaviors to cope with the fear of flying.

CLASS 1

Of the fifty people who gathered one winter evening in the meeting room at Logan International Airport, about half were newcomers. The rest were graduates of earlier classes who had started a club of former flight-phobics called "Logan's Heroes." The graduates, who shared a bond of camaraderie, like soldiers who had gone through battle together, were on hand this night to lend moral support to the new class.

The group was about evenly divided between men and women, whose ages ranged from the early twenties to the late fifties. They were a diverse group: bearded young men in dungarees, executives in business suits, professional women, suburban housewives, and some grandmotherly types. Nevertheless, they all shared one common feature: the fear of flying.

Sitting in the meeting room, Ted could look through large picture windows and see planes taking off and landing every few minutes. Jets roared overhead, and the screech of tires at the moment of touchdown could be heard. Ted was not aware that he had already taken three very important steps toward overcoming his fear of flying: he had openly admitted that he was afraid to fly; he had made a decision to try to rid himself of this fear; and he had begun, the process of systematic desensitization by driving to the airport, entering the terminal building, and exposing himself to the sights and sounds of flying.

A large part of the first class was directed toward establishing a strong motivation for completing the program. Members of Logan's Heroes took turns describing the problems that flight fear had created for them and how their lives had been enriched by overcoming the fear. Such testimonials as these were typical:

"We used to live in L.A., and when we moved to the East I thought I'd never see my friends again because I was so scared of flying. I wasn't really sure the class would help me, but my husband persuaded me to try it. What can I say? I'm flying now, and it's fine. I really enjoyed my last trip to L.A."

"I always felt before every trip that I was never coming home again . . ."

"I was sure I would be the program's first failure, but I went through with it . . . and here I am."

"We went back to the hotel where we had spent our honeymoon. I hadn't seen it for 29 years."

"I can remember what I was thinking the first night I started the class. Several people got up and talked about how they had overcome their fear. I remember thinking to myself, they probably were not as scared as I was. But I know now that they were. I can assure you that when we started the class, those of us who are talking to you tonight were every bit as scared of flying as you are right now."

A young man with long blond hair announced that he had even started taking flying lessons after completing the course, and the group applauded loudly. As the stories were told, Ted realized that he was far from alone. The other newcomers to the class were just as afraid to fly as he was and just as ashamed of showing their fear.

Another method of motivating the class members was less direct. Two flight attendants in full uniform helped with some of the formalities and served coffee and pastries part way through the evening. In addition, the room had been decorated with colorful travel posters that beckoned to far-off and exotic places. The blue waters and sunny beaches of the Caribbean looked particularly appealing that wintry night.

A therapist explained to the class that fear of flying typically involved not one but several fears, including claustrophobia, fear of heights, fear of loud noises, and fear of losing control and appearing ridiculous. A few nervous giggles greeted his stories of the woman who was afraid that she couldn't go to the bathroom on the plane, and the man who was afraid of moving inside the plane for fear that it would tip over. Then, the class members were invited to tell why they were afraid to fly. The reasons included the following:

"I'm concerned with human error."

"I don't like being up there where I can't get out. I'm not in control."

"I feel very helpless."

"I sometimes worry that the pilot may have been drinking."

"I start worrying about all sorts of things because I figure once the real trauma starts, I won't have time for it."

"I'm afraid of my own fear reactions."

Ted R. could identify with many of the reasons given. He felt better simply knowing that he was neither unique nor alone in his feelings toward flying.

The final part of the evening was devoted to a brief review of some statistics on aircraft safety.

"More people are killed each year by being hit by lightning than in plane crashes.

"In 1974, 55,000 people were killed in highway accidents; 20,000 people died from falls; 2,600 people were accidentally shot to death; 1,500 people died when their automobiles were struck by trains; 7,400 deaths were attributable to boating or drowning accidents.

"By contrast, only 135 people died in crashes of commercial airliners.

"Insurance rates, which reflect the odds of being killed in an airplane crash, have declined steadily in the last decade: from $1 per $5,000 of flight insurance to 50¢ per $25,000 of flight insurance.

"In 1969, a person flying in a commercial airliner had a 99.99992 percent chance of safely completing the journey (100 percent would mean absolute certainty of safe completion). And safety records are improving steadily by almost any measure you choose to consider."

Acknowledging that such statistics would have very little impact on a person's ability to deal with fear, the therapist pointed out that the statistics should at least be reassuring. Since people were safer in an airplane than in their own homes, and certainly safer than in a car, their fear of flying was clearly disproportionate to the actual danger.

For Ted and the others, the first meeting was as much a social event as a class. But it served its purpose. In a subtle way, a tiny bit of the threat of flying was chipped away. It was the first step in a process of associative learning, the initial link in a chain of associations through which Ted would begin to learn new expectations and new behaviors with respect to airports, airplanes, traveling, and his own fear.

CLASSES 2–4

In the second class, the technique of rating fears using subjective units of discomfort (SUD) was introduced. As students rated their feelings about being airborne on the SUD scale in the manner described in Chapter 5, the numbers were entered into a small calculator. The sum of the ratings divided by the number of people in the class gave an average SUD rating of just over 50. Ted was slightly above the class average with a level of 60.

Next, the class was introduced to progressive muscle-relaxation techniques like those described in Chapter 4. The therapist spoke the instructions rather than use a recorded tape. Practice sessions were repeated, and, after each session, they assessed their SUD ratings. By the end of the second class, the average SUD level reported was in the mid-twenties. Ted had lowered his rating to 30. Class members were advised to set aside twenty to thirty minutes a day to practice the muscle-relaxation exercises in a quiet setting.

At the beginning of the third class, the average SUD level was in the low forties, an improvement of some 10 points over the beginning levels of the previous week. In addition to muscle relaxation, the class members were introduced to the guided-imagery techniques and thought-stopping. By the end of the exercise periods, the average SUD level was down in the low twenties. Ted's level was 25.

Typically, the first part of a class was devoted to relaxation exercises, and the second part concentrated on familiarizing students with various aspects of airplanes, airline safety, and air travel. A tour of the airport was arranged, giving class members the opportunity to receive a detailed overview of the airport's operations and facilities. Members watched a travel movie in which people were seen enjoying themselves aboard the plane and in a Caribbean resort. While the film familiarized class members with certain airline procedures, it also provided strong images of people who were relaxed and happy in connection with flying. As such, it served to create positive feelings associated with flying.

Another short movie explained how air-traffic controllers work. By focusing on the strict training that controllers undergo and the high standards they must meet, the film helped to instill an understanding and appreciation of the heavy emphasis on safety in the airline industry. Afterward, a control supervisor explained to the class the elaborate precautions taken to ensure maximum safety and described the sophisticated equipment employed in takeoffs and landings. The supervisor was a soft-spoken man who exuded self-confidence and competence, thus making a highly favorable impression.

The familiarization part of the program had two goals. First, it was intended to demystify flight procedures and create an understanding of what is involved in the whole complex business of moving people through the air safely and comfortably. Second, at the same time, it helped to create an environment in which fewer conscious processes would be required to attend to exterior stimuli so that a larger part of the conscious capacity could be devoted to relaxing.

By the beginning of the fourth class, the opening average SUD level had dropped to the high thirties. Ted's level was 35. An unplanned sequence of events helped to demonstrate the effects that the relaxation exercises were having. Midway through one of the early practice sessions, a young woman was stricken with severe abdominal pains. While one of the therapists continued the exercises, another therapist attended to the stricken woman. She had to stretch out on the floor for a few minutes, but then she recovered and continued with the class.

A few minutes later, a large travel poster taped to the wall became unstuck with a loud ripping sound, which caused everyone in the room to jump. As one of the flight attendants hastened over to fix it, she tripped over the projection screen, which slammed into the wall with another astonishingly loud noise. All the while, the exercises continued. When they were complete, the average SUD level had dropped 17 points to a new low for the class—19.

As the average SUD levels came down, another learning technique was brought into play. Previous graduates of the class had booked a charter flight to Bermuda, and it would be open to members of the present class. Ted was especially intrigued by the idea: it could mean a chance to get away with his wife for a few days. Such a tangible reward provided new incentive and reinforcement. In addition, the graduation flight, which earlier had been regarded as the final grueling test of nerves, was increasingly viewed as something to look forward to. It could be a reward for a job well done, complete with champagne and a great view.

As part of the continuing familiarization process, a supervisor of ground services spoke on aircraft safety maintenance, putting it in a framework that had personal meaning for each class member. He likened aircraft maintenance to automobile maintenance in this way:

"Suppose you decided that you wanted to take care of your car as carefully and thoroughly as we take care of a plane. What would you have to do? To start with, you'd need three full-time mechanics who would check out every inch of the car every time you drove it, whether you just went to the grocery store or drove across the country. You would have to replace the tires every 500 miles and have a complete tuneup every 2,500 miles. Every 10,000 miles, the mechanics would take the engine completely apart, overhaul it, replace any worn parts, and use X-rays to check key components for excessive wear. Every 25,000 miles, you would have a completely new engine installed.''

The supervisor cited statistics showing that three-quarters of a million dollars were spent each year to maintain a single aircraft in top shape. For a fleet the size of Pan American's, 3.5 million dollars a day are spent just on aircraft maintenance. He pointed out that, for each hour a plane spends in the air, it spends five hours in maintenance on the ground.

His final point was this: ''Airline pilots are not considered to have hazardous occupations. They pay the same for life insurance as bank tellers. That's pretty safe!''

CLASSES 5—9

When Ted arrived at the fifth meeting, he discovered a new seating arrangement. The chairs had been placed in a long column with three chairs on either side of a narrow aisle. This pattern simulated the way the class would sit in an airplane, and the class members were instructed to think of it as a plane. Understandably, people had to be reminded several times that walking through the walls of the plane was not allowed.

Class members treated the exercise as something of a game—which it was. But it served its purpose. It represented a further step toward the eventual situation the class would encounter in actual flight. It was also a way of involving imagination in the practice of exercises. And so, during the next five classes, this same seating arrangement was used for the relaxation practices. At each new class session, additional details were added to more closely simulate the actual flight conditions.

For example, a flight attendant made the routine announcements—required by law to be given before each flight—concerning location of emergency exits, operation of oxygen masks, and other safety precautions and procedures to be followed in an emergency.

At the next class, a tape recording was used to provide the full sequence of sounds that occur during takeoff. The therapist ran the tape through, explaining:

"After taxiing out to the main runway, you will hear a sharp increase in the engine noise. The plane will begin to roll forward, quickly gathering speed. You will feel yourself being forced against the back of the seat. As the plane lifts off, you may feel a slight pressure in your buttocks. When the plane is safely in the air, you will hear a grinding noise as the landing gear retracts, and then a loud thump as it locks into place. This is a normal part of all flights."

With the class seated in the simulated aircraft and the tape-recorder sounds giving the effect of a takeoff, the relaxation exercises were conducted. As new details were added to the flight simulation, the SUD level would rise slightly, but would then drop back with the relaxation exercises.

By the ninth class, SUD levels were in the teens through low twenties even with complete flight simulation, from boarding through emergency instruction, greetings from the captain, and very realistic takeoff sounds on the tape recorder. At times, the therapist would lead the exercises; at other times, class members would conduct the exercises on an individual basis.

From the fifth class on, at every meeting the therapist

would explain at least once the overall procedure that would be followed leading up to the graduation flight:

"The last class will be held in the departure terminal. We will conduct relaxation practices in the departure lounge. We will file through the entry ramp and actually go aboard the plane. We will take seats, and I will conduct another relaxation session there. Everything will be done exactly as we will do it on the actual flight, except that we will not fly that evening.

"On the day of the actual flight, we will repeat these procedures: starting in the departure lounge, boarding the plane, and taking a seat. I will ask your permission to close the door. If there is anyone who does not feel comfortable and confident about the flight, I will not close the door. The plane will not take off without your approval. Each of you individually will be in complete control of the situation."

Ted R. found that the repetition of these instructions helped shape his expectations. He found it reassuring that he would not be surprised. He was also relieved to know that he would not be forced to fly against his will.

Throughout the classes, the familiarization process continued, both in the simulation of flight conditions and in the form of educational presentations. A pilot spoke to the group about the training and testing that pilots undergo to receive accreditation to fly commercial airlines. He emphasized that pilots are required to undergo frequent physical checkups to ensure good health, and that regulations strictly limit the number of hours that pilots can fly, to ensure against fatigue.

The class visited a small local airport on a Saturday morning. There, they had the opportunity to see small planes, talk with private pilots, and learn about the oper-

ations of the facility. The visit served partly as familiarization and partly as a reward for progress in the form of a
weekend outing to someplace new and a little different.

CLASS 10

The final class was held in the departure lounge of the Pan
American terminal at Logan International Airport. The contrast between this meeting and the first class was inescapable.
The atmosphere was festive, and Ted joined in, laughing and
talking. He enjoyed meeting in a new place with so much
activity. Planes roared outside, the public address system
crackled with endless announcements, and passengers rushed
to their flights, hunted for baggage, and frantically tried to
find out what gate they were supposed to go to—all the usual
sights, sounds, and frenzy of going on a trip.

The class gathered at a departure gate not in use, and the
therapist led them through the relaxation exercises. Repeated
checking of SUD levels after each run-through of muscle
relaxation and guided imagery showed small but steady
decreases in overall anxiety. Before entering the plane, the
group received a last-minute instruction from the therapist:
"As you go down the loading tunnel, you may find yourself
slightly disoriented. The tunnel slopes down gradually; it's
not your imagination. The passageway is narrow, and the
ceiling is low, but you don't have to worry about bumping
your head; it's not that low. Noises sound strange in the
tunnel, so don't be surprised if voices take on a different
sound or you hear echoes. It's all supposed to be
happening."

Armed with this final bit of advance information, Ted filed
onto the plane. Two people ahead of him stumbled slightly,
thrown off balance by the slight pitch of the loading ramp.

They were instructed to hold a hand against the wall to overcome disorientation.

The therapist stood in the doorway checking SUD levels. People called out their levels in high spirits: "Twenty-five," "Twenty," "Twenty-five," "Thirty." Had anyone's level been above 30, he or she would have been asked to wait outside and perhaps to go through another round of relaxation to bring down the level. But that didn't happen. Ted's level was a reasonably calm 15.

Aboard the plane, the laughter and chatter had stopped. It was quiet except for the busy clicking sounds of people experimenting with seat belts. The therapist conducted a short version of the relaxation exercise and then asked, "Do I have your permission to close the door?" No one objected.

The door was closed. The therapist explained the slight increase in cabin pressure, which Ted had noticed. He advised people to yawn, swallow, or chew gum to help equalize the pressure.

The final advice was: "Don't obsess. Don't think about next Sunday's forthcoming flight. Don't ask yourself, What am I getting into? Use thought-stopping techniques if you find yourself dwelling on it. Be sure to get a good night's sleep before the flight. We want you here well rested."

Then Ted walked out of the plane. The class was finished. All that remained was the final exam.

THE FLIGHT

The morning of the flight found Ted and his fellow class members in a serious mood. Unlike the last class when he knew he would not be flying, Ted knew this was the real thing. His conversation was more subdued. There was some nervous laughter around him. However, even though concern was apparent, there was clearly no panic on anyone's part. Just before the relaxation exercises were to start, Ted looked across the room at a cluster of passengers waiting to board. With surprise, he remarked, "They look more scared than we do."

The initial SUD rating showed no one's level to be over 50. Ted had a level of 45, and a few other class members had levels in the forties. The rest were in the thirties, and a few were even lower. After the first exercise, the highest ratings were 35—and there were only two of those. Everyone else— Ted included—had a lower level.

The flight captain spoke briefly to the group to reassure them. His manner was easy and confidence-inspiring. A jovial, robust man with a trace of gray at the temples, he could hardly have been more suitable for the part had he been cast for a Hollywood movie. "Don't worry about the weather," he said with a smile, "because I'm not going to."

The relaxation exercises continued right up to the moment of boarding the plane. Everything was carried out exactly as it had been rehearsed in the last class. The only difference was that, this morning, the plane would take off.

The therapist asked permission to close the door. Permission was granted. The exercises started again and continued as the plane taxied out to the runway. When the plane took off, it was hardly any different from the practice sessions. The element of actual motion had been introduced, but Ted was expecting it and was prepared.

The cheer that went up when the captain announced that they were airborne expressed a great sense of pride and achievement. People who had never before flown—except in silent terror, clutching the armrest—were now up and moving about. It was a party. Everyone was allowed into the cockpit to look at the complex array of instruments and to see the view below from the best seat in the plane.

Midway through the one-hour flight, the plane hit some turbulence. The sign to fasten seat belts flashed on, and most smiles vanished. Even so, there was no panic. The pilot announced that the turbulence was both mild and routine. The therapist suggested that anyone who felt a rise in anxiety should go through the relaxation process.

The relaxation exercises were repeated just prior to landing, and just before touchdown a final SUD rating was taken. The class average was a laudable 18.8. Ted's level was 15. For him, it was one of the happiest landings of his life.

13.
CHILDREN'S FEARS

Like all mammals, human children are small and helpless at birth. For quite a few years, a child's very survival depends almost entirely upon people who are older, stronger, and supposedly wiser. Because of this dependence, young children are highly vulnerable when left alone—a fact they seem to recognize almost instinctively. The cry of a child left in the crib is an effective survival technique. It offers a strong reminder: "Don't forget me and leave me here." A fear of being left alone has survival value in a child's early life; however, like other adaptive fears, it can be transformed through learning experiences into disproportionate fears in later life.

Every day, hour after hour, new experiences—new sights, sounds, tastes, and smells—bombard the newborn at what must be a bewildering pace. The infant's vulnerability is increased by such constant exposure to change and newness. As the child grows and develops new abilities, additional sources of novel experience occur in terms of what the child can do and the changes that the muscles, brain, and related faculties are undergoing. Undoubtedly, some of these new experiences will be startling or unpleasant. As such, they create fear-learning processes in the young child.

At some point in the child's early development, the marvelous human faculty of imagination becomes active. It is from imagination that human creativity and achievement originate. However, when combined with infantile vulnerability and constant change, imagination is a potent ingredient of fear. Young children lack the ability to reason about what is likely or even possible; they lack the firsthand experience that enables one to differentiate what can actually happen from what can be imagined. In the absence of logic and experience, which put bounds on adult imagination, children's thoughts are free to wander without limits. Forays into the uncharted wilderness of an unimpeded imagination are bound to produce some frightening thoughts. And the stronger the imagination, the greater the fear.

The combination of vulnerability, novelty, and imagination make it inevitable that children will have fears. Fears are not a "weakness," as some people believe, but an unavoidable part of growing up. They are natural, normal, and, in many cases, healthy. For, without appropriate fears, little boys and little girls alike would succumb to accidents and bad judgment long before they became adults.

Many non-adaptive childhood fears are outgrown as mental, physical, and emotional development takes place. But given an unfortunate combination of learning experiences, some of these fears can become disproportionate—they can persist and grow and become problems in later life.

How parents—and society in general—respond to a child's fears becomes a major conditioning factor in the child's learning experiences. The goal of this chapter is to identify some of the common fears experienced by virtually all children, to examine the factors that influence how children react to these fears, and finally to indicate the appropriate parental responses to children's fears. If you have children of your own, the framework of understanding that we present here, linked with sensitivity toward your child as an individual may help you to be a better parent. If you don't have children, you may still find this chapter useful in learning to recognize and cope with the fears of the child within each of us.

TEMPERAMENT AND ENVIRONMENT

Each child is born with a certain temperament, a physical or biological constitution that is reflected in his or her level of activity and responsiveness. Through temperament, children are predisposed to behave in particular ways. Just as there are happy babies and cranky babies, there are also anxious ones and calm ones. A child's temperament has tremendous impact on development. It influences not only how the child will react to stimuli, but also how parents, siblings, peers, and society in general will react to the child.

As early as the first few weeks of life, infants discover that they can exert an influence on the world through their individual actions. They begin to learn behaviors that allow them to extract from the world what they want: food, closeness to mother and father, dry diapers, and so on. Through their ability or inability to manipulate the world in a satisfactory way, they develop varying degrees of independence and self-confidence—traits that will play major roles in shaping their personalities, their responses to the outside world, and their methods of dealing with fear.

While temperament predisposes the child to behave in certain ways, the child's environment to a large extent determines what stimuli will be presented for the temperament to act upon. The interaction of temperament and environment may be likened to an artist's selection of material for a painting. The type of paints to be used depends on the surface to be painted: water colors for certain papers, pastels for others, and oils for canvas. The child's temperament is the "surface," ready to accept some paints and not others. The "paint" is the environment that overlays the surface to give form and color. The "artist" is the parent who recognizes the advantages and limitations of the materials at hand and skillfully blends them to produce a rich and varied work of individual distinction.

In the child's early life, the most important aspect of the environment is parental attention, or the lack of it. As the child grows older, objects assume more importance: a favorite blanket, a teddy bear, clothes. Gradually, other people assume more of a role, and playmates—the peer group—become dominant factors in the child's environment. No amount of parental intervention can shape a fear-free environment for a young child. The wisest and most sensitive parent can hope for no more than to create a climate in which children's fears are neither given undue weight nor dismissed out of hand, neither nurtured nor suppressed. Like bumps and bruises, fears are part of the price that a child must pay to move into the ever unfamiliar territory of adulthood.

Children of dependent temperaments are especially prone to fears of novelty in the environment or of being separated from parents. Such fears become apparent when Mom and Dad try to go out for the evening, when the child is sent to school, or when the child is reluctant to try new and different things. To avoid these fears, parents often work to instill a greater sense of independence. Children of independent temperament may learn to cope adeptly with separation fears and novelty in the environment. However, they are more likely to develop fears of being out of control, or of being overwhelmed by powers, real or imagined, outside their control. Usually, children will be dependent in some situations and independent in others. The fears they display will reflect this mix of temperaments in accordance with the environmental influences to which they are subjected.

A well-adjusted child is not fearless. Therefore, any parent who sets a goal of eliminating a child's fear is unrealistic and certain to fail. The child with the best chance of becoming a well-integrated adult is the one who has opportunities to accept the closeness and companionship that comes from dependence on family and friends, while being encouraged to make the independent choices and judgments that are so essential to individual self-realization. The fortunate child is one who receives the love, support, and understanding of parents throughout the ages and stages of childhood fears.

FEARS AND THE MATURATION PROCESS

In the first few months of life, infants show little or no ability to recognize one person from another. They tend to react about the same way to anyone who approaches them gently. But at five to six months, babies tend to cry and show other signs of discomfort when around strangers. At the same time, the child also becomes able to distinguish between the presence and absence of the mother. Psychologists regard these signs as evidence of two early childhood fears that are so common that they are virtually universal: fear of strangers and anxiety over separation from parents.

Psychologists are by no means certain about how or why these early fears start. Some believe that the basic separation anxiety is an instinctual outgrowth of the infant's vulnerability when left alone. Attempts have been made to explain fear of strangers as an extension of the separation anxiety—that is, the presence of a stranger may signal the absence of the parent. Other theories have contended that fear of strangers is simply one of the earliest examples of fear of anything new, unfamiliar, or unknown. Whatever the reasons for these fears, it is certain that they form the basis for certain aspects of the child's subsequent experience.

The child's physical and mental development present a whole range of new and unfamiliar situations as grist for the fear mill. Utterly harmless events are suddenly transformed into fearful situations when the new-found power of imagination, unfettered by reason or experience, combines with anxieties over separation or unfamiliar stimuli. Children learning to walk find suddenly that they possess the power to bring about the feared separation under their own steam and are capable, by themselves, of introducing vast new realms of unfamiliar and potentially frightening experiences. With the development of language comes a new capacity for memory and expectation, both essential ingredients in the learning of fearful behaviors.

Puberty is an especially fertile time for the growth of fears. The child's body changes rapidly and visibly, becoming a source of novelty, wonderment, and anxiety. At the same time, strong new feelings and sexual urges develop. Prior to the onset of puberty, children do not experience such intense emotional changes; thus, nothing can truly prepare them for these changes. Many of the sexual mores of the Western culture intensify the difficulties of puberty, and thus give rise to a wide range of fears that can lead to impotence, frigidity, and other sexual dysfunctions.

Figure 13-1 shows how childhood fears change with growth and development. Five common fears are shown in terms of their frequency of occurrence in children up to five years of age. Fears of noises and associations, strange situations, and injury are fairly common in very young children, but decline steadily as the children acquire in-

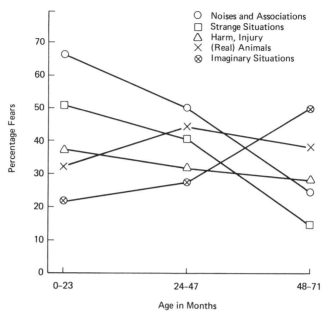

Figure 13-1. The relative frequency of fear responses in children of different ages. (Reproduced from *Phobias, Their Nature and Control*, S. Rachman, Charles C Thomas, 1968.)

creased control of their own lives, depend less on parents, and can fend for themselves better. Fears of real animals increase during the first two years, at about the same rate as fears of imagined situations, suggesting that imagination could play a role in animal-related fears. However, after two years of age, these fears begin to drop off, and fears of imagined situations rise very sharply. It is during this time that the child's imagination is developing rapidly and the constant flow of new experiences is providing a wealth of raw material for imagination to work upon.

In a study similar to the one summarized in the figure, the reactions of children between the ages of two and six were studied in such situations as being left alone, exposure to sudden noises, dark rooms, strange persons, high places, and sights of dogs and snakes. Overall, the largest percentage of children who showed fear were in the two-to-three-year-old age group, with the greatest number of fearful responses being shown toward dogs (61 percent) and to dark rooms (46 percent). Three-to-four-year-olds responded fearfully only slightly less often and showed greater fear of the dark and of snakes than did the younger children. By four to five years of age, the percentage of children showing fearful response had dropped markedly, with dogs, snakes, and dark rooms still provoking fearful responses most often. In the five-to-six-year-old age group, no fearful responses were observed except for snakes, which still frightened 30 percent of the children, and dogs, which frightened 12 percent.

Reasons suggested for the decline in fears after age six include the child's growing ability to reason, to understand cause-and-effect relationships, and to distinguish between fact and fancy. For example, plumbing drains and vacuum cleaners, with their ability to make things disappear, are sometimes the objects of childish fascination and fear. When children gain the ability to distinguish between what sorts of things can and cannot be legitimately "disappeared," fear of these devices usually vanishes. A child who hears Mom complaining that "ants eat everything" may be understandably wary of ants until he acquires additional information about the world, which then allows a more realistic appraisal. A child's inability to think in any terms but concrete, literal ones may provide the basis for stories that are funny to adults but that may well be no laughing matter to the child.

While childhood fears specifically focused on an object or situation tend to vanish, other fears of a less specific nature may take their place: anxieties over social status, fear of rejection, fear of failure. Some of these fears are generated entirely by the child; others may be hand-me-downs from adults. In either case, children, like adults, will tend to avoid what they fear, to hide their fear, and to suffer quietly the loss of self-esteem that it brings. In a real sense, fears create problems by forcing us into childish patterns of behavior, which are not necessarily made any more agreeable when they happen to afflict children.

THE PARENTS' RESPONSE TO CHILDREN'S FEARS

Faced with the inevitability of children's fears, what can a parent do? First, recognize that your child has an individual temperament, and try to understand what it is. Realize also that it is not totally consistent, for a child may be independent at certain times, dependent at others. It is important for a parent to understand how the child's temperament interacts with the environment. While recognition of a child's inherent limitations is essential, these limitations should not set absolute limits on behavior. Rather, a recognition of limitations should provide suggestions as to how parents should help a child cope with fear. An outgoing child who does not seem frightened by novelty might not require as much attention in the face of new situations as a child who is frightened easily. When confronting a possibly fear-provoking situation, a parent should attempt to break the fearful situation down into smaller parts, the size of which depends upon the temperament of the child.

A child who has already developed a fear can be treated in much the same way as an adult would. Gradual exposure to the fear situation combined with strong positive reinforcement of nonfearful behavior is, by far, the best way to deal with childhood fears. Children respond favorably to gradual desensitization. A slow learning experience, in which the child is brought closer to a feared object or situation, will often help the child to overcome a particularly difficult fear.

The sink-or-swim approach, in which a child is forced to confront a frightening situation all at once, should never be used. While such an exposure, known in psychological terms as *flooding,* may possibly work, there are inherent dangers with this technique. Basically, if a child escapes the fearful situation before becoming completely comfortable in it, then the entire pattern of fearful behavior in relation to that situation will be reinforced. For example, a child exposed to a dog may begin to cry fearfully. When the dog does not bite, the child will eventually get tired of crying and calm down. But if the child is taken away from the dog before becoming calm, the fear will be reinforced. The child may lose confidence in his own abilities and in the adult who forces the situation. Desensitization is *always* preferable to flooding.

In helping a child overcome a certain feared object, parents can achieve good results by introducing the object into the room while the child is occupied with some pleasant activity, such as eating. Over a period of time (minutes, hours, days or weeks, depending on the child and the situation), the object can be brought closer. The child should be kept comfortable all the time that he or she is in the presence of the feared object. Another good approach is to let the child observe other children playing with the feared object in a nonfearful way. Research has shown that learning through observation is an extremely powerful phenomenon, which can be harnessed as an extremely effective therapy.

In the case of separation anxiety, a child can be gradually conditioned by being left alone for increasing periods of time. One good technique is to go out of the child's room for a few seconds and then to return before he or she starts to cry; then, reward the "good" behavior with affection and attention. Gradually increasing the periods of absence followed by a reward of affection can help a child learn that separations are neither forever nor unpleasant. However, to continue to stay whenever the child starts crying can prolong the anxiety stage and impede the child's progress toward independence.

While fearful behavior should definitely not be rewarded, neither should it be punished. Punishment serves only to create new anxieties. Deception is not a good idea either: if little Oscar learns that Mommy has foisted him off on a babysitter after she has promised to be there while he naps, little has been accomplished to build the trust and confidence he needs to deal with fears.

The fear of dark rooms can usually be alleviated with a small compromise on the parents' part. Leave the door open a crack, or get a small night-light. A favorite blanket or teddy bear can lend security and help with the problem. As with other desensitization approaches, the amount the door is left open or the illumination of the night-light can gradually be decreased over a period of months until the child is comfortable sleeping in a completely dark room.

A word of caution: don't overrespond to minor, normal, transient fears. An overresponse, with the best of intentions, can have the opposite effect—that is, it can reinforce a fear rather than extinguish it. Children quickly learn to manipulate parents by claiming fear. If such claims prove to be a useful means of bending the world to their will, children will continue to employ them with possible bad effects in the long run.

Remember, fears are a normal part of growing up. Given love, affection, and support, children will outgrow most fears—unless they receive reinforcement (in the form of additional attention and special consideration) each time they claim to be afraid. A little common sense and the simple techniques explained in this book will go a long way toward preventing minor fears from becoming excessive.

However, be aware that professional help is available for children whose fears are severe or resistant to extinction with age. Seeking professional help for a child in need of it is *not* a sign of failure either for you as a parent or for your child. It most often represents a healthy and open admission that the combination of the temperaments and environment of both child and parents is in need of a tuneup.

PRIMARY PREVENTION OF FEARS

Up until now, we have been discussing how fears emerge and how parents can keep small fears from becoming larger. This is known as *secondary prevention*. There has been a considerable amount of psychological research on the *primary prevention* of fear—that is, preventing fears from occurring in the first place. Much of this research has focused on children.

In approaching children's fears, it is important to remember that gradual exposure and explanation of a novel experience can go a long way toward defusing a possible fear related to that experience. Children who must face a potentially threatening new experience, such as a first admission to a hospital, a prolonged separation from a parent, or a minor surgical procedure, can benefit by having their parents explain to them in advance exactly what is going to happen to them. One good practice is to take children to the place in which the fear may occur *before* the fear situation actually arises. For instance, if a child must undergo some medical procedure in a hospital, then the parent should first show the child the hospital and, if possible, the rooms in which the child will undergo treatment. If the child is old enough to understand, the parent should explain what the hospital is all about and the procedures that the child will encounter. Much mileage toward preventing a fear can be gained by allowing children to express any emotions that they may have about the upcoming event. Simply because they are not quite sure how to present it, parents sometimes create fearful situations by failing to explain a situation to their child.

Children's fears, like adult fears, are frequently learned responses. Some children's fears are innate, but many others are developed through a process of classical conditioning—that is, the association of a nonthreatening (but novel) situation with some sort of trauma. Research has shown that fears resulting from classical conditioning can be prevented if a child is given sufficient experience with the situation beforehand. For instance, modern dentists who specialize in treating children will show a child all of the equipment in the dental office before any actual treatment. The appearance and sound of the drill and other dental instruments are not frightening in themselves. However, because they may later on become associated with discomfort, they have the potential of becoming powerful stimuli for evoking fear.

Experiments on both animals and humans have shown that fear learned by association can be inhibited if the stimulus to which a person is likely to become afraid (such as a dental drill) is repeatedly preexposed before it is associated with any trauma. Children who have had the good fortune to spend many hours horseback-riding before their first fall are much less likely to become afraid of horseback-riding than are those who fall early in their riding career. The more positive experience that occurs with any situation before a trauma occurs, the more resistant children are going to be to developing a fear to that situation.

Another type of primary prevention can be accomplished by careful attention to the type of models a child is exposed to. Modeling, or learning through watching other people, is one of the most powerful learning experiences. Children model the behavior of their parents as well as that of their peers. If children see their parents exhibit fearful behavior, they can easily develop the same behavior. For instance, children's fears of animals are often learned from parents. A mother who is afraid of flying may think that she is able to disguise her fear, but the child may well pick up her true attitude and model the fearful behavior. Parents would do well to deal with their own maladaptive fears simply to ensure that they do not pass them on to their children. A child's peers can also play a key role in instigating fears. A child will sometimes develop a new fear for which the parent has no obvious explanation. Sometimes the child's playmates are exhibiting the same fear. In such cases, the fear of the whole group of children may have to be dealt with before the particular child can learn to overcome the new-found fear.

The psychologist Erik E. Erickson calls childhood the time when we learn whether or not the world is a satisfying place in which to live. If proper experience can be used to deal with learned and unlearned fears—both to prevent them and to teach children how to cope with them—children will be far more likely to develop into adults who can cope easily with new experiences. Children who can cope with fear are more likely to develop trust in themselves, in their ability to master the environment, and their ability to trust others. The greater the trust, the wider the range of emotional responses over which a child is capable of reacting. This, in turn, results in an openness to new experiences that reduces the opportunities for fears to develop, and enhances the child's ability to cope effectively with the realities of adult life.